THE ULTIMATE BOOK
of WEDDING CAKES

THE ULTIMATE BOOK

of WEDDING CAKES

LESLEY HERBERT

MEREHURST

DEDICATION
To my husband, Tony, with all
my love. This year we celebrate
our twentieth wedding
anniversary – I wish the brides
who look at this book the
happiness we share.

Published in 1994 by Merehurst Limited, Ferry House,
51-57 Lacy Road, Putney, London SW15 1PR
Text copyright © Lesley Herbert 1994
Photography and design copyright © Merehurst
Limited 1994

Reprinted 1994

ISBN 1 85391 251 4

Designed by Maggie Aldred
Edited by Bridget Jones
Photography by Clive Streeter
Colour illustrations by Nicola Gregory
Colour separation by Fotographics, Hong Kong
Typeset by Litho Link Ltd., Welshpool, Powys
Printed by G Canale & C Spa, Italy

CONTENTS

USING THIS BOOK

The cake designs are intended for those who are
familiar with basic skills and various techniques. At the
beginning of each cake, the techniques are displayed in
a 'skills' box. Each cake is also graded and the level of
competence in sugarcraft required to complete the
design is indicated by the following symbols.
Remember that the skills can be interchanged – or
sometimes specific decorations omitted – according
to your ability, to create a variety of different
designs at all levels.

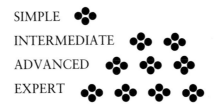

SIMPLE

INTERMEDIATE

ADVANCED

EXPERT

INTRODUCTION

Creating the cake of a lifetime calls for time,
patience and an artistic approach to design to
ensure the result lives up to the occasion.

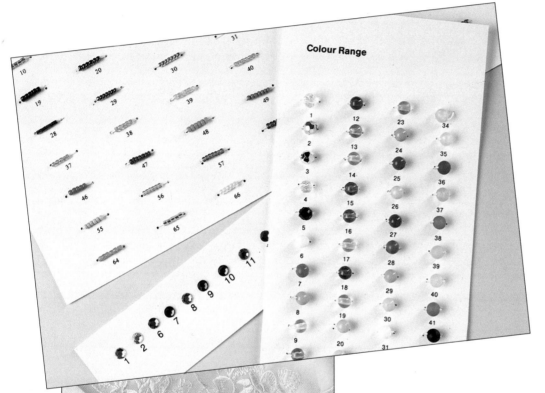

The wedding cake, or bride cake, plays a traditional role in the marriage celebration and, alongside the bride and groom with their attendants, it is a focal point for the wedding breakfast, especially during the cake-cutting ceremony. The bride is often helped in selecting the design by her mother or a friend but she will usually seek the advice of the cake decorator who will be putting her ideas into practice. Deciding on the perfect combination takes careful consideration and expert guidance is important. Wedding themes are popular, with a deliberate choice of style echoed in all aspects of the celebration. A colour scheme is always important and this is reflected in the dresses, flowers, table decorations and other trimmings. As well as planning the colour for the cake, the bride may wish to pick up on other style features. The cake may be quite traditional in many respects but with variations in the shape of stand or with unusual details of decoration to add a personal touch.

The bridal gown is always an excellent source of inspiration for the cake design. Lace, beads, fabrics and their finishes can all present ideas for decorative touches which can be used on the cake.

Ask the bride for details of the flowers or a consultation with the florist is a good idea when there are specific themes to follow through. The florist will provide exact details of the flowers and a colour sample to match. Fresh flowers may form part of the cake design, in which case they should have a long drink of water for at least 12 hours before they are wired and taped into bouquets so that they stay fresh and beautiful throughout the reception.

The cake decorator should have a good understanding of the reception. The numbers of guests and the layout of the reception room are essential information to consider when estimating the size and shape of cake. The position for displaying the cake is important – for example, a tall cake should not be placed directly in front of the bride and groom where it will be distracting during the speeches or it may conceal the happy couple. Tall tiered cakes make the greatest visual impact in a large hall or room where low displays can look insignificant and lost.

Many unusual cake stands are available to enhance the cake and they often have the added advantage of providing a safe display platform which dispenses with the risk of the cake collapsing under its own weight.

This book is designed for

brides to browse through and make a selection as well as to inspire the competent cake decorator. It is anticipated that the colours will be selected according to the bride's wedding theme and the shapes of the cakes may be varied or designs interchanged

to provide a broad range of possibilities.

Producing a stunning wedding cake is the ultimate ambition of all cake decorators. I hope it will give you the confidence for executing individual ideas.

WEDDING ROMANCE

A romantic cake with a
bell-shaped top tier supported
on a lace-covered pedestal. Delicate
peach-coloured piped roses and hearts make
an attractive border on this modern wedding cake.

SKILLS
~
Piped shells
Piped roses
Textured frill
Piped embroidery

small bell-shaped cake
25cm (10 inch) round 7.5cm
(3 inch) deep cake
15cm (6 inch) and 33cm
(13 inch) round boards
nos. 44, 1, small petal and
O piping tubes (tips)
straight frill cutter
double scallop crimper
7.5cm (3 inch) length of
7.5cm (3 inch) diameter
perspex tube, covered with
30cm (12 inch) lace

▲ Coat the cakes with
marzipan (almond paste) and
white sugarpaste, then allow
the coating to dry for 3 days
before decorating the cakes.
Cut a 10cm (4 inch) circle of
greaseproof (parchment)
paper, fold it in half then into
six equal sections and cut the
convex scallop shape from the
edge. Pin this pattern over the
top of the bell and scribe the
design. Scribe a straight line
3cm (1¼ inch) from the board
around the base of each cake.
Pipe a shell border around the
base of both cakes using a no.
44 piping tube (tip).

8

◀ Cover the heart templates, see page 144, with cellophane. Using runout icing and a no. 1 piping tube (tip) pipe a large shell to form half of the heart, place under a warm lamp until partially dry, then pipe the other half of the heart. Make 24 hearts. Cut six 5cm (2 inch) lengths of ribbon and fold each piece just over halfway along its length. When they are dry, remove the hearts from the cellophane and attach to the ribbon ends with dots of icing.

For the heart decorations: 24 hearts and 2.2m (2½ yd) × 3mm (⅛ inch) ribbon.

▶ Roll out the sugarpaste 3mm (⅛ inch) thick and cut out the frill using a straight cutter. Trimmings from covering the cake will be sufficient for making the frill. Emboss equally spaced lines in the frill using a cocktail stick (toothpick).

▼ Dampen the cake below the scribe line. Lift the frill onto the cake taking care not to distort the lines. The shell border supports the frill at an angle. Crimp the frill top.

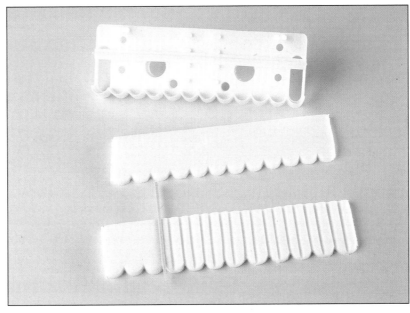

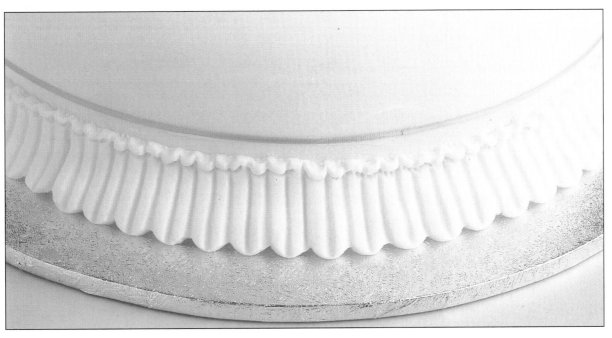

▶ Using a no. 0 piping tube (tip) and soft-peak peach coloured royal icing, pipe groups of three dots randomly on the top of the bell. Pipe tiny dots in the spaces between the groups of dots.

◀ Divide the round cake into six equal convex-scalloped sections and use dots of royal icing to attach pairs of hearts to the side of the cake between the sections. Attach pairs of hearts to the points of the scribe line on the bell cake. Make six small ribbon bows and secure them to the round cake. Complete the cakes by securing the roses in place on the scallop marks, using the buds on the round cake. Pipe small shells to represent leaves at each end of the sprays of roses.

Pipe 36 peach roses, and 12 rosebuds using full-peak royal icing and a small petal tube.

BRIDAL BLOSSOMS

A royal-iced wedding cake with appliqué flowers and butterflies. Surrounded by sprays of sugar flowers, the crystal butterfly decorations on each tier make charming gifts for the bridemaids or prominent wedding guests.

SKILLS
~
Oriental string work
Cut-out flowers
Piped shells
Moulded flowers

15 × 10cm (6 × 4 inch) oval
5.5cm (2¼ inch) deep cake
20 × 15cm (8 × 6 inch) oval
6cm (2½ inch) deep cake
25 × 20cm (10 × 8 inch) oval
7.5cm (3 inch) deep cake
15 × 10cm (6 × 4 inch),
29 × 15cm (8 × 6 inch) and
25 × 20cm (10 × 8 inch) thin
oval boards
23 × 18cm (9 × 7 inch),
28 × 23cm (11 × 9 inch) and
33 × 28cm (13 × 11 inch) oval
boards
nos. 0 and 1 piping tubes (tips)
blossom cutters
small butterfly cutter
3 crystal butterflies
three-tier metal cake stand

Place the cakes on thin boards cut to their exact sizes. Coat the cakes with marzipan (almond paste). Coat the cakes and boards with white royal icing. Secure the cakes to the boards. Fill any space between the cakes and boards with royal icing. Secure a band of 3mm (⅛ inch) ribbon around each cake base.

2m (2¼ yd) × 3mm (⅛ inch) ribbon.

▲ Cut strips of paper the same height and length as the cake sides. Fold each into six equal sections. Mark the oriental string work pattern on each section. Divide the pattern into portions not larger than 3.5cm (1½ inches) long and mark the divisions with a dot at the top and bottom edges. Fold in half lengthways. Draw the stem around the pattern middle. Trace the pattern onto the paper back using a H pencil. Scribe on the cake.

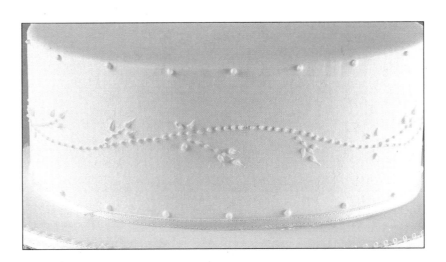

► Use a no. 0 piping tube (tip) and apple green royal icing to pipe small shells for the stem and leaves. Use a no. 1 piping tube (tip) and softened royal icing to pipe rows of dots on the top and bottom edge where marked.

◄ Cut out four hundred blossoms in tints of pink, lilac and white. Thread stamens into one hundred for the top decoration. Using a small cutter, cut out twenty four white butterflies. Attach small groups of flowers to the stems on the cake sides with dots of icing. Brush the butterflies with lustre dusting powder (petal dust/blossom tint) and attach them.

About 125g (4 oz/¼ lb) flower paste and 100 stamens.

► Pipe the string work using a no. 1 piping tube (tip), taking loops of royal icing from dot to dot. The loops should not touch the side of the cake. Allow to dry. Turn the cake upside down, then pipe a second row of loops around the top and bottom edge. Dry. Turn the cake the right way up. Repeat several times, alternately using green and white icing and making each row of loops slightly shorter than the previous row.

► For the top decoration, make a long rope of flower paste, lay it on the curved shape and dry it flat. Cut out one 4cm (1½ inch) circle and three 2.5cm (1 inch) circles from finely rolled flower paste. When dry secure the base of the curved rope to the large circle and attach two small circles to the ends to make the stand. Allow to dry. Wire bunches of blossom to 28 gauge wire and make some small ribbon loops. Place a small piece of flower paste on the remaining circle. Make a small posy of ribbons and flowers. Carefully attach the posy to the stand. Trim the base of the stand with cut-out blossom and attach the crystal butterfly with a little royal icing to keep it firmly in place.

2.4m (2¾ yd) × 5mm (¼ inch) ribbon for board edge.

Pipe dots of royal icing to attach the sprays of flowers and crystal butterflies to the top of each tier.

BRIDAL BELLS

This fairytale wedding cake sparkles
from top to bottom as it catches
the light. The lily bouquets
are filled with diamond-centred
small white flowers to complement
the diamanté trimming on the extension work.

SKILLS
~
Piped shells and dots
Bridge and extension
work
Piped loops
Moulded flowers

three 18cm (7 inch) medium
bell-shaped cakes
23cm (9 inch) large bell-shaped
cake
three 25cm (10 inch) round
boards
30cm (12 inch) round board
4 posy holders
no. 0, 1 and 2 piping tubes
(tips)
perspex cake stand

▲ Coat the cakes with
marzipan (almond paste) and
white sugarpaste, and insert
posy holders. Dry for 3 days.
Scribe a line around each
cake, 3.5cm (1½ inches) from
the board. Mark small holes
around the cake, 5mm
(¼ inch) above the board and
2.5-3.5cm (1-1½ inches) apart
for the bridge work.

▲ Pipe the embroidery using a
no. 0 piping tube (tip) and
white royal icing to pipe
groups of three circles. Use
pale apple green royal icing to
pipe three small shells to
represent leaves around each
group of circles. Pipe a shell
border around the cake bases
using a no. 1 piping tube (tip)
and white royal icing.

▶ Using a no. 2 piping tube (tip), pipe four rows of bridge work loops. When the icing is dry, pipe another two rows of loops using a no. 1 piping tube (tip). It is important to keep each row of icing directly on top of the previous row. When the piped bridge work is dry, paint it with softened royal icing to neaten and strengthen it. Cut the diamanté into strips and extend them from the bridge work to the cake, attaching both ends with dots of icing.

About 3.6m (4 yd) diamanté (including flower centres).

◀ Pipe the extension work using a no. 0 piping tube (tip) and fresh, well-beaten royal icing. Pipe four small loops above the extension work between the strands of diamanté. When dry, drop another loop of icing to link pairs of loops and to form a lace effect.

▲ Make four shower bouquets and one crescent bouquet for the top tier, wiring the flowers together to drape around the bells. Place the bouquets in the holders.

Make 15 cream lilies and 8 lily buds, 25 variegated ivy leaves and 125 small pulled flowers, half with stamens and the remainder with diamond centres.

SWEET ENCHANTMENT

Subtle shades of one colour enhance the
beautiful extension work and large
full-flowering rose blooms on this
three-tier oval cake.

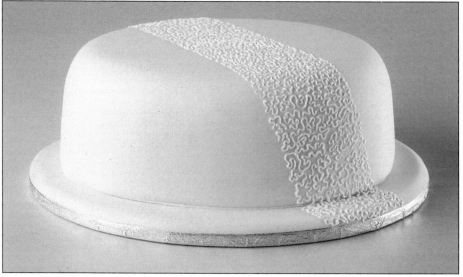

15 × 10cm (6 × 4 inch) oval
5.5cm (2¼ inch) deep cake
20 × 15cm (8 × 6 inch) oval
6cm (2½ inch) deep cake
25 × 20cm (10 × 8 inch) oval
7.5cm (3 inch) deep cake
15 × 10cm (6 × 4 inch),
20 × 15cm (8 × 6 inch) and
25 × 20cm (10 × 8 inch) thin
boards
20 × 15cm (8 × 6 inch),
25 × 20cm (10 × 8 inch) and
33 × 28cm (13 × 11 inch) oval
boards
nos. 0, 2 and 1 piping
tubes (tips)
low staggered stand

▲ Place the cakes on thin
boards cut to their exact size
and coat with marzipan
(almond paste). Coat the
cakes and boards with peach-
coloured sugarpaste. Allow to
dry for 3 days. Secure the
cakes to the boards. Cut
strips of paper for the filigree
pattern. Pin them diagonally
over the cake tops and sides,
and down over the boards.
Scribe lines around the middle
of the cake sides. Mark small
holes 5mm (¼ inch) above
the boards and about 3cm
(1¾ inch) apart for the bridge
work pattern.

▲ Pipe the filigree work using
a no. 0 piping tube (tip) and
white royal icing. Pipe a small
shell border around the base
of the cakes up to the filigree
work.

A photograph can only indicate the
beauty of this cake which must be
seen in reality to be appreciated.

► The bridge work consists of four rows piped using a no. 2 piping tube (tip) and two rows using a no. 1 piping tube (tip). Note that the bridges on each side of the filigree work are shaped by reducing the length of each successive piped line added to the bridge. Cut 3mm (⅛ inch) wide ribbon into 1cm (½ inch) lengths for the ribbon insertion. Mark the positions for the ribbon around the scribed line – use dividers set open at 5mm (¼ inch). Cut slits in the sugarpaste coating on the marks, then insert the ribbon pieces.

About 2m (2¼ yd) × 3mm (⅛ inch) ribbon.

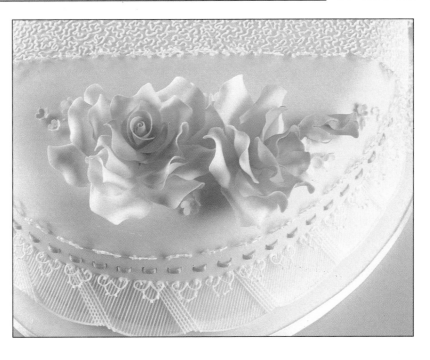

◄ Tilt the cake towards you. Pipe extension work using a no. 0 piping tube (tip), 5mm (¼ inch) below the ribbon insertion. Pipe another two rows of bridge work using a no. 0 piping tube (tip). Tilt the cake diagonally and pipe five lines of extension work to each bridge peak. Use a no. 0 piping tube (tip) to pipe three hundred pieces of lace. Dry and attach as shown.

300 lace pieces.

► Finally, attach the flowers as shown on each tier. Soften some flower paste with water, place it in a paper piping bag and pipe a small amount on each flower to secure it to the cake. Trim the board edges.

Make 6 fully blown roses, 5 rosebuds and about 60 peach and white blossoms of various sizes. 2.6m (3 yd) × 5mm (¼ inch) ribbon for board edges.

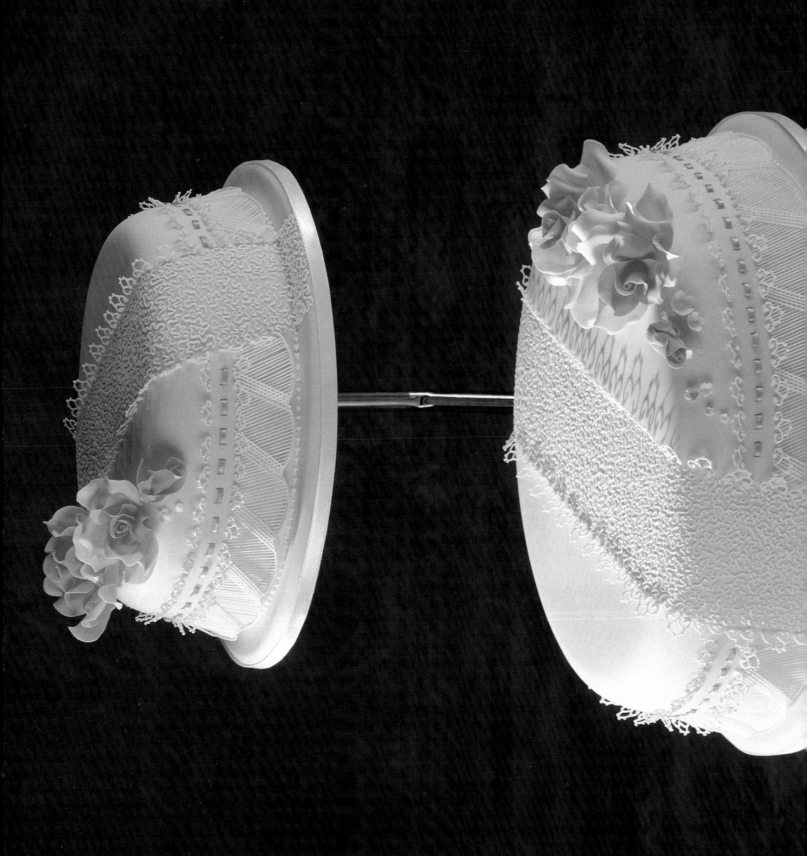

ELEGANCE

An unusual-shaped cake with delicate art

work and piping, this two-tier design

is best displayed on an angled

stand to set off the decorated top

tier to best effect.

SKILLS

~

Painting
Brush embroidery
Edible ribbon insertion
Piped embroidery
Graduated line piping
Bridge and extension
work, single and double
Moulded flowers

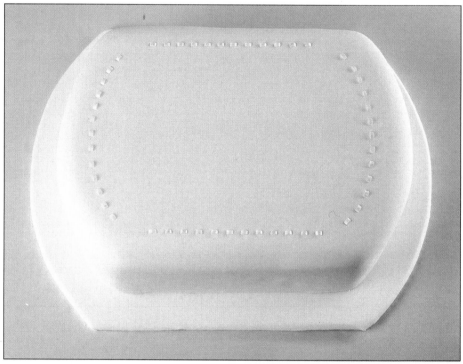

30cm (12 inch) round 7.5cm
(3 inch) deep cake
16 × 11cm (6½ × 4½ inch)
rectangular cake
boards, see method
30cm (12 inch) round thin
board
nos. 1, 2 and 0 piping
tubes (tips)
tilting perspex stand

Cut sugar ribbon from 3mm
(⅛ inch) wide strips of flower
paste, each 5mm (¼ inch)
long. Dry them over greased
wooden dowels. Dust with
white luster dusting powder
(petal dust/blossom tint).

About 125g (4 oz/¼ lb)
flower paste.

▲ Cut a piece off each side of
the round cake. Cut the top
of the rectangle cake into an
arch using a card template as
a guide.
Place the cakes on thin boards
cut to their exact sizes. Coat
the cakes with marzipan
(almond paste), then coat
them and the boards with
pale lemon sugarpaste. Cut a
template 3.5cm (1½ inch)

smaller than the diameter of each cake. Place on top of the cakes and use as a guide to insert the prepared ribbon pieces evenly. Allow the cakes to dry for a week. The boards are specially cut for the cakes. The board for the bottom tier is 3.5cm (1½ inch) larger than the coated cake all around. The arch-shaped board is 2.5cm (1 inch) larger around than the coated cake, on all sides. Secure the cakes to the boards.

Cut a strip of paper the same length and height of the base cake side. Draw the extension work design, making each loop no wider than 3.5cm (1½ inch). Note that the curved ends of the cake have two rows of extension work as shown on the template, see page 145.

Place the template around the cake and scribe the design. Prepare the pattern for the arch cake, keeping the extension work as equal in size to that on the base cake as possible; ensure that the front corners are symmetric. Scribe the designs on the cakes. Place a small shell border around the base of each cake using a no. 1 piping tube (tip). The bridge work consists of four rows of line work, piped using a no. 2 piping tube (tip) and two rows piped directly on top of each other using a no. 1 piping tube (tip).

◄ Turn the cake upside down and pipe the graduated line work using a no. 1 piping tube (tip), taking care to ensure that the points of each scallop are in line with the bridge work. Turn the cake back the right way.

▼ Pipe the bottom layer of extension work using a no. 0 piping tube (tip) and well-beaten, fresh royal icing.

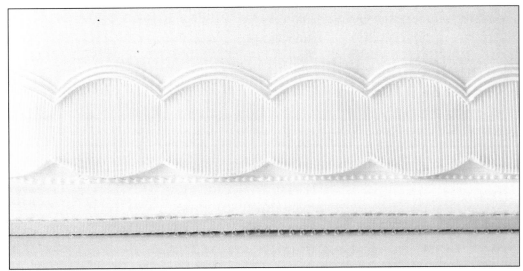

This cake does not have any artificial decoration, so it is completely edible.

► Turn the cake upside down and pipe the second layer of bridge work, using the same piping tubes (tips) and number of loops as for the first bridge work. Complete the extension work using a no. 0 piping tube (tip). Tilting the cake slightly towards you will help to give straight piped lines and prevent sagging.

▼ Scribe the bride picture, see page 144, on the arched cake. Paint the background, groom and bride's face with food colouring, diluting the colours with water or clear alcohol. Brush embroider the bride's dress and veil using a no. 1 piping tube (tip), beginning with the areas which appear furthest away. Pipe dots of icing using a no. 0 piping tube (tip) for the bride's bouquet

and use the same tube for the embroidery between the ribbon insertion. Add sprays of blossom and yellow roses.

5 yellow roses, 10 yellow rosebuds and about 25 blossoms.

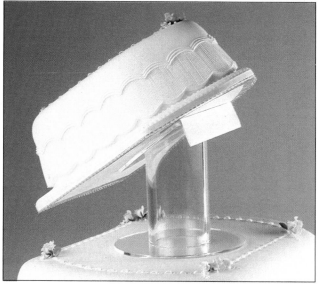

▲ Cut a short length of plastic right angle strip (available from D.I.Y. and hardware stores) and glue it to the back of the arched board, positioned to hook over the stand so that the cake is displayed at an angle. Trim the board edges with ribbon.

1.8m (2 yd) × 5mm (¼ inch) picot ribbon.

CRYSTAL TIERS

Beautiful cut-crystal rose bowls support the three tiers of this cake, trimmed with rosebuds and sugar bows above the delicate piped border. This is the perfect cake for a glorious summer wedding.

SKILLS
~
Filigree piping
Line piping
Cut-out bows
Moulded flowers

13cm (5 inch) round 5.5cm
(2¼ inch) deep cake
20cm (8 inch) round 6cm
(2½ inch) deep cake
28cm (11 inch) round 7.5cm
(3 inch) deep cake
20cm (8 inch), 28cm (11 inch)
and 36cm (14 inch) round
boards
no. 1 piping tube (tip)
bow cutters
3 cut-crystal glass rose bowls
3 small round mirrors

Coat the cakes with marzipan (almond paste) and white sugarpaste. When the coating is firm, secure the cakes to the boards with a small amount of royal icing.

▶ Cut a strip of greaseproof (parchment) paper the same length and height as the side of each cake. Fold the paper into six equal portions and trace the design on page 144 onto each section. Pin the pattern in place on each cake in turn, taking care to ensure that all the pencil marks are on the outside of the paper. Scribe through the paper to mark the design lightly.

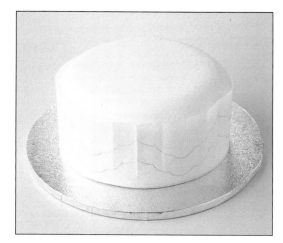

▼ Use a no. 1 piping tube (tip) and white royal icing, pipe a small shell border around the base of each cake and pipe drop loops over the scribe lines. Pipe the filigree using a no. 0 piping tube (tip).

▶ The zig-zag and scallop design are piped using a no. 1 piping tube (tip), working from left to right.

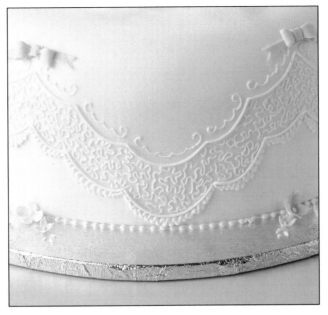

▼ Use the appropriate size bow cutters to make six flower paste bows for each tier. Attach the bows to the cakes with royal icing while the paste is still pliable.

▼ The cakes are supported on rose bowls. To distribute the cake's weight, each bowl is placed on a mirror on the cake. Secure sugar roses and blue daphne around the mirror with royal icing. Complete the cakes with sprays of three daphne and piped leaves on the board.

25 unwired roses and 125 cut-out pale blue daphne.

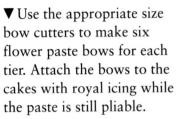

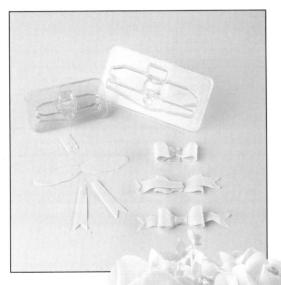

◀ Tape a piece of dry flower oasis into the rose bowl for the top decoration. Assemble the wired roses and daphne sprays into the oasis to form a dome shape. It is important to push some of the flowers close to the oasis to fill the gaps and prevent the oasis from showing.

About 24 wired roses and 30 sprays of daphne.

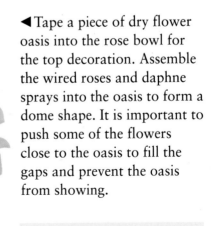

CRYSTAL TIERS

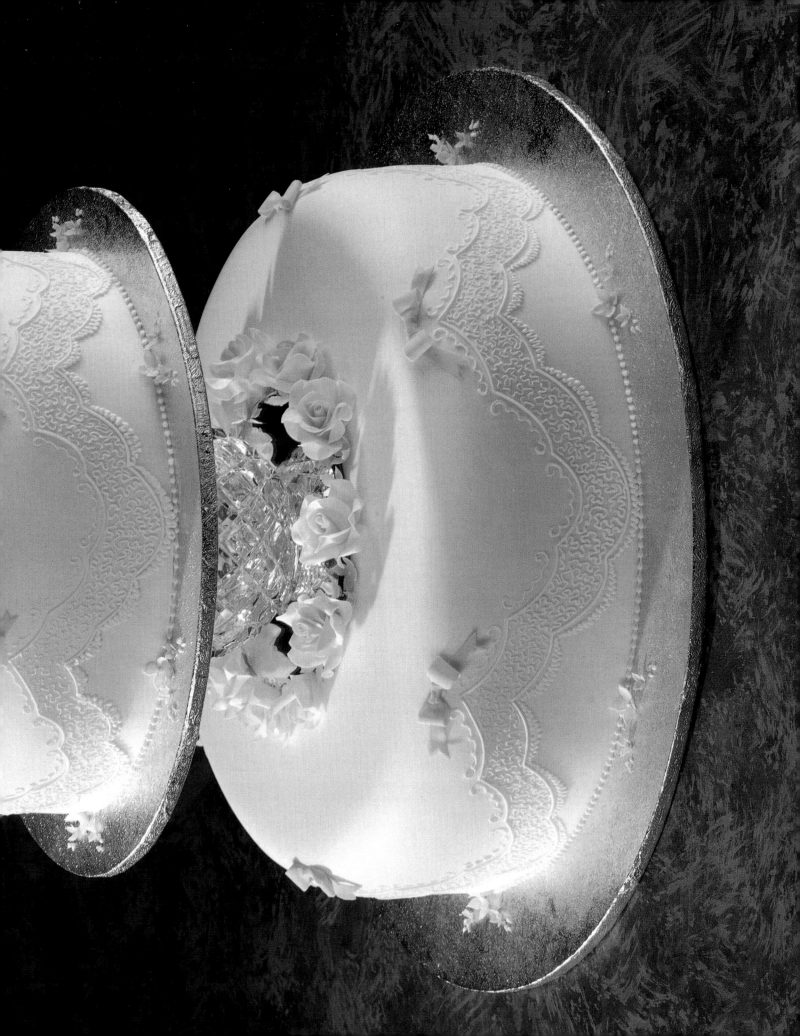

CLASSIC EMBROIDERY

Lace and bridal fabrics used for the bride's dress were the inspiration for the elegant embroidery decoration on this cake. The patterns were simplified so that they could be piped in icing. The clear pillars and delicate roses were designed to co-ordinate with the bridemaids' gowns and to enhance the overall wedding theme.

SKILLS
~
Piped embroidery
Moulded flowers

15 × 23cm (6 × 9 inch)
scalloped oval 6cm (2½ inch)
deep cake
23 × 30cm (9 × 12 inch)
scalloped oval 7.5cm (3 inch)
deep cake
23 × 30cm (9 × 12 inch) and
30 × 38cm (12 × 15 inch)
scalloped oval boards
nos. 1 and 0 piping tubes (tips)
4 perspex pillars
perspex vase

▶ Coat the cakes with marzipan (almond paste) and white sugarpaste. Dry for 2 days. Cut a strip of greaseproof (parchment) paper for each cake: the same height as the cake and long enough to fit around the side. Trace the pattern, see page 145, on the strips of paper – it may be necessary to adjust the length of each scallop to make the design fit accurately. Pin pattern in place on each cake in turn. Take care to keep all pencil marks on the outside of the paper. Scribe the design on the cake.

▼ Remove the pattern. Using a sharp pointed tool, make small holes of different sizes in the sugarpaste over the scribe marks to form the lace design.

► Pipe a small shell border around the bottom of the cakes using a no. 1 piping tube (tip). Using a no. 0 piping tube (tip) pipe the embroidery and brush embroider the flowers to finish the border design. Mark the position for the pillars on the bottom tier. Insert the dowels in the cake, see page 140. Trim.

▼ Using a no. 0 piping tube (tip), pipe groups of three small circles randomly on the top of the cakes to complete the embroidered-fabric effect. Trim the board edges with wide and narrow ribbon.

2m (2¼ yd) each of 5mm (¼ inch) and 3mm (⅛ inch) wide ribbon.

Pick out the main elements on a complicated fabric design to make a pattern which can be piped in royal icing.

► Each spray of roses consists of one large rose, two buds and two leaves, secured in place with royal icing.

For the flower spray: 8 large roses, 16 rosebuds and 16 rose leaves, all without wires.

◄ For the top decoration, wire the roses together with the leaves to form a posy, filling in with the white filler flowers and ribbon loops to complete the shape. Wire in four trailing ribbons, then stand the posy in the vase.

For the vase of sugar flowers: 10 roses, 12 white filler flowers, 12 rose leaves and ribbon loops.

ANTIQUE ROSE

The simple pattern creates a quilting

effect on this diamond-shaped cake.

Matched with piped pearls

and the deep colour of the silk roses,

the design imparts an antique appearance

to the cake which is ideal for winter weddings.

SKILLS
~
Embossing
Piped shells
Simple painting

20 × 10cm (8 × 4 inch)
diamond-shaped 6cm
(2½ inch) deep cake
30 × 18cm (12 × 7 inch)
diamond-shaped 7.5cm
(3 inch) deep cake
38 × 25cm (15 × 10 inch) and
28 × 18cm (11 × 7 inch)
diamond-shaped boards
tile spacers
no. 1 piping tube (tip)
costume jewellery rings
celtiers cake stand

▲ The diamond pattern is
made by using plastic tile
spacers to emboss the soft
sugarpaste coating. The tile
spacers are readily available
from do-it-yourself stores and
hardwear shops. Cut the
plastic spacers with small
sharp scissors, to give the
large and small imprinted
diamond design.

This cake highlights the fact that
simple designs can be most effective.

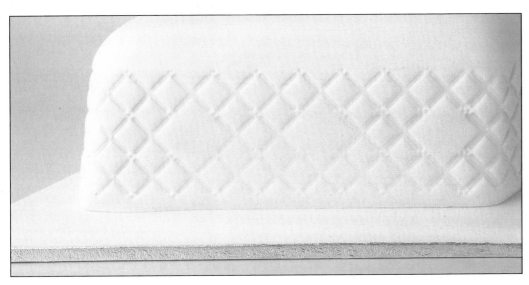

◄ Coat the cakes with marzipan (almond paste) and ivory-coloured sugarpaste. Using double-sided tape, stick the cut tile spacer to a piece of clear perspex. Position the diamond carefully at the front corner of the cake and gently emboss the sugarpaste. The diamonds at the front of the cake must be accurately aligned. Allow to dry. Coat the boards in ivory sugarpaste and position the cakes.

► Paint a tear-drop shape of white food colouring in the required diamond shapes, as shown, and outline the left side of each with black food colouring. Pipe a shell of clear piping gel in each tear drop to make the small crystal droplets. Pipe a dot of gel in the centre of each large diamond.

◄ Pipe a small shell border around the cake base using a no. 1 piping tube (tip) and four shells around the piping gel in each large diamond to form a flower. Edge the boards with ribbon. Attach the roses and leaves to the cake boards with royal icing.

24 silk rose leaves, 40 silk roses in ivory and burgundy, some dried gypsophila and 3.2m (3½ yds) × 5mm (¼ inch) pico edge ribbon.

ANTIQUE ROSE

▲ Make the two flower sprays. Cut out two 4cm (1½ inch) circles of flower paste or pastillage and allow to dry. Attach a marble-sized ball of sugarpaste to the circles, then push the stems of the flowers into the soft paste. Make small bows of ribbon with long tails. Use tweezers to finish assembling the sprays. Attach the flower sprays and two wedding rings to the cakes with royal icing.

WEDDING DAY

Teddy bears are always a favourite with young brides. The cake sides feature a little photographer and bridesmaids, and the top decoration of the bride and groom teddy bears in a hand-painted arch complete the light-hearted, appealing theme on this fresh-looking cake.

SKILLS
~
Runout figures
Runout collars
Piped lines and dots
Painting
Cut-out pastillage

13cm (5 inch) round 6cm
(2½ inch) deep cake
20cm (8 inch) round 7.5cm
(3 inch) deep cake
13cm (5 inch) and 20cm
(8 inch) round thin boards
20cm (8 inch) and 30cm
(12 inch) round boards
no. 1 and 0 piping tubes (tips)
3 round chalk or plaster cake
pillars

▲ Cut off about a quarter of each cake to create the required shape. The cut cake can be given to the bride as a sample and it will show how well the cake will cut. Place the cakes on thin boards cut to their exact shape and size. Then coat them with marzipan (almond paste).

Coat the cakes and boards with white royal icing.

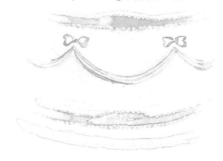

▶ Trace the templates on page 146 and make the two top and two bottom runout collars, using a no. 1 piping tube (tip). Allow them to dry under a warm lamp. Pipe a picot edge around the outside of each collar using a no. 0 piping tube (tip). Remove the dry bottom collar from the wax paper and secure it to the board with softened royal icing. Place the white collar on top securing it with dots of royal icing.

The small amount of blue decoration makes the white icing on this cake appear brighter and it lightens the classic, basic design.

▶ Cut a strip of greaseproof (parchment) paper the same length and height as the curved portion of the cake side. Fold the paper into twelve equal sections then cut a quarter circle into it; place around the cake. Following the pattern, pipe three rows of graduated line work using a no. 1 piping tube (tip). Secure cake to the board with royal icing. Fill in any small gaps between the collar and cake with softened royal icing.

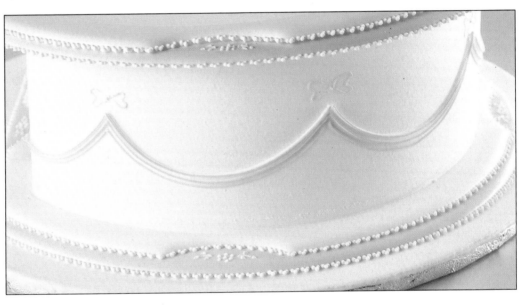

◀ Runout the bears and mice, see page 145. Leave to dry then paint the details with food colouring. An advantage of having a flat front on the cake is that the runouts do not have to be dried over a tin to curve them. Attach the runouts to the front of the cakes with dots of royal icing.

► Use softened icing to stick pairs of top collars together; dry. Attach to the cakes with softened icing. Trim the board edges with lace.

About 1.8m (2 yd) lace.

Use a no. 0 piping tube (tip) to pipe dot flowers on collars. Pipe two blue hearts for bows on the sides of the cakes.

▼ Cut top decoration from finely rolled pastillage using a cardboard pattern, see page 145. Dry the arch back over a bottle. Trace, scribe and paint the pictures on the arch with food colouring.

About 125g (4 oz/¼ lb) pastillage.

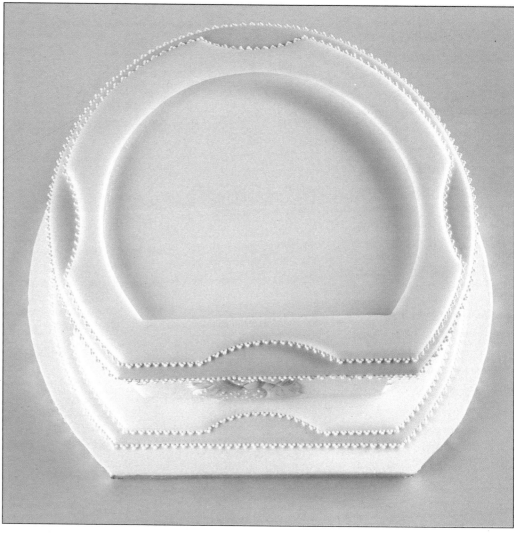

Position the painted run-out bears on the top tier, place a small amount of icing under their feet and support with foam or sponge until dry. Position the arch and secure the little painted doors with royal icing. Pipe a few dots of royal icing around the arch to anchor it on the cake.

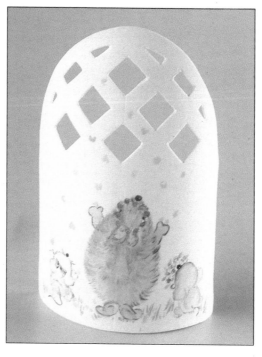

SPRING GARLANDS

Garlands of lemon and violet flowers fall gracefully from the top of this exclusive seven-tier wedding cake which is sure to delight any spring bride.

SKILLS

~

Bridgeless extension work
Picot dots
Piped embroidery
Moulded flowers

10cm (4 inch) and 13cm
(5 inch) round 5cm (2 inch)
deep cakes
15cm (6 inch) and 18cm
(7 inch) round 5.5cm (2¼ inch)
deep cakes
20cm (8 inch) and 23cm
(9 inch) round 6cm (2½ inch)
deep cakes
25cm (10 inch) round 7.5cm
(3 inch) deep cake
16cm (6 inch), 18cm (7 inch),
20cm (8 inch), 23cm (9 inch),
25cm (10 inch), 28cm
(11 inch) and 33cm (13 inch)
round boards
7 posy holders
nos. 1, 00 and 0 piping
tubes (tips)
cake stand: fabric-covered
wooden dowels set into
wooden base

▲ Coat the cakes with marzipan (almond paste) and white sugarpaste. When the coating is dry, secure the cakes to the boards with a small amount of royal icing. Fill any gaps between the cakes and boards with royal icing and attach the ribbons around the cake bases.

About 5m (5½ yd) × 3mm (⅛ inch) yellow ribbon.

▲ Cut a strip of greaseproof (parchment) paper the same height and length as the side of each cake. Fold the patterns into six equal sections. Trace a heart, see page 147, on each fold. Draw curved lines between the tops of the hearts for the extension work. Mark equally spaced dots between the bottom of the hearts: two dots on the five smaller cakes and four dots on the two largest cakes. Trace this design onto each folded section of the pattern.

Place the pattern around the cake and scribe only the scallop line and pin marks onto the paste, not the hearts. Place the cakes on the stand and mark the positions for the bouquets, then insert the posy holders, in place.

▶ Use a no. 1 piping tube (tip) to pipe the hearts on wax paper, see page 147. Allow to dry. Remove the piped hearts using a cranked pallet knife. Tilt the cake forward, support the hearts in place on pins inserted in the coating. Pipe two dots of icing where the hearts touch the cake and allow to dry before carefully removing the pins.

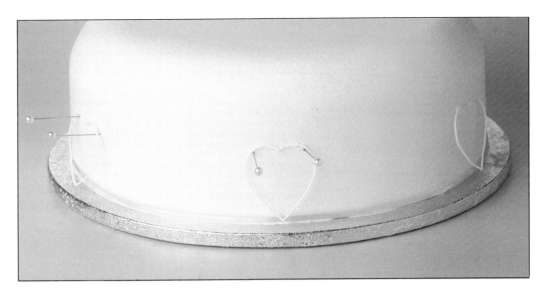

▼ Position pins in the marked points between the hearts. Paint each pin with vegetable fat. Use a no. 1 piping tube (tip) to drop a loop over the pins, between the hearts.

Pipe the extension work using a no. 00 piping tube (tip) and well-beaten royal icing. Remove the support pins as the extension work is finished. Carefully fill in the pin holes with royal icing, removing excess with a brush.

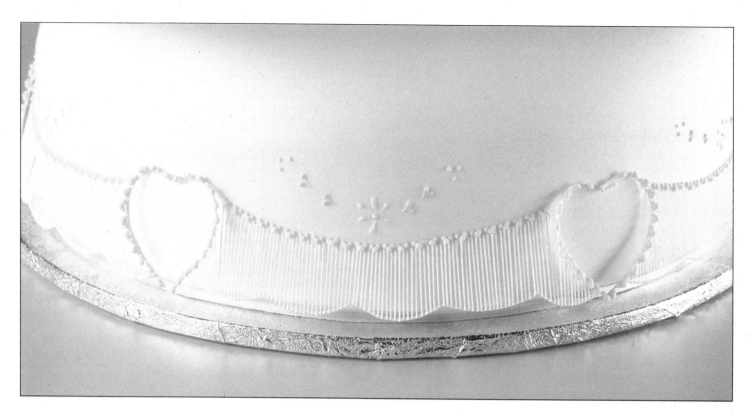

▲ Use a no. 0 piping tube (tip) and soft yellow icing to pipe a picot edge around each heart and along the top of the extension work. Using the template on page 147, pipe the embroidery design in violet and lemon icing using a no. 0 piping tube (tip).

The delicate extension work design, inset with yellow-trimmed hearts, makes this a once-in-a-lifetime cake.

▲ Prepare the flower bouquets in advance. Each bouquet has a similar number of flowers but they are graduated in size as they are made to suit the different-sized cakes. Each bouquet contains about fourteen yellow roses, fourteen ivy leaves, fourteen sprays of violet daphne and twelve sprays of white blossom.

About 100 yellow roses, 100 ivy leaves, 100 sprays of violet daphne and 85 sprays of white blossom.

WITH THIS RING

Hoops of flowers and butterflies on a crystal ring symbolize love and eternity on this colourful cake. Layers of petticoat frills and crystals create a design that is visually appealing even from a distance – the ideal cake for displaying in a large wedding reception venue.

SKILLS
~
Petticoat frills
Piped shells and dots
Cut-out hearts
Moulded flowers

13cm (5 inch) round 5.5cm
(2¼ inch) deep cake
20cm (8 inch) round 6cm
(2½ inch) deep cake
28cm (11 inch) round 7.5cm
(3 inch) deep cake
13cm (5 inch), 20cm (8 inch)
and 28cm (11 inch) round thin
boards
20cm (8 inch), 28cm (11 inch)
and 36cm (14 inch) round
boards
round frill cutter
medium and small heart cutters
6 long perspex pillars
perspex ring for top piece

▲ Place the cakes on thin boards, cut to their exact sizes and coat with marzipan (almond paste). Coat the cakes and boards with white sugarpaste. Allow to dry for 3 days. Secure the cakes to the boards and fill any gaps with royal icing. Use a no. 1 piping tube (tip) to pipe a small shell border around the base of each of the cakes.

Cut a length of paper to fit around the side of each cake, then fold each into six equal sections. Draw the loop shape for positioning the frill accurately on each portion. Mark the embroidery pattern, see page 147, making a pin hole for the centre of each flower; do not mark the hearts. Scribe the pattern on the cake.

Trim the board edge. Cut out the petticoat frills using three shades of aquamarine sugarpaste and a round cutter. Attach the frills to the cake with water, then trim their ends level with a scalpel, following the scribed line.

2.6m (3 yd) × 5mm (¼ inch) ribbon.

►Make the white frill and attach it to the cake above the petticoat frills. Trim the top of the frill level using a scalpel, then dry. Use royal icing to attach the crystal drop beads above the frill; support with pins. Remove pins when dry.

4m (4½ yd) strong crystal-drop beading.

◄Cut out six medium and twelve small peach sugarpaste hearts per cake and attach with water. Pipe dot flowers using a no. 1 piping tube (tip).

Mark the divisions for the pillars either in line with the side design points or between alternate loops. The long pillars go through the cake and support the tiers. Remove a core of icing, marzipan and cake, then insert a pillar straight down.

▼ Use floristry tape and a length of 24 gauge wire to make three ropes of flowers long enough to form rings around the pillars on the middle and bottom tiers. Bend hooks in both ends of the wire; shape into rings.

Make 100 sprays of peach and aquamarine blossoms in various shades and 50 small pulled peach flowers with stamen centres. Wire 200 sprays of dried gypsophila.

▲ Cut-out three butterflies, see page 147, from flowerpaste and allow to dry. Paint the details on them with food colouring. Assemble the butterflies with royal icing. Lay the perspex ring down flat and stick the butterflies in place, supporting them with tissue until dry.

BELLS *of* JOY

This is a delightful cake for a small wedding or wedding anniversary. Garlands of pastel-coloured piped flowers and hearts encircle the painted bells and tiny teddy bears. An inscription can be piped on the cake top to personalize the design.

SKILLS
~
Painting
Piped embroidery
Piped bulbs

25 × 20cm (10 × 8 inch) oval
7.5cm (3 inch) deep cake
25 × 20cm (10 × 8 inch) oval
thin board
33 × 28cm (13 × 11 inch) oval
board
nos. 0 and 3 piping tubes (tips)

▲ Place the cake on a thin board of its exact size. Coat the cake with marzipan (almond paste) and white sugarpaste. Coat the board. Allow to dry for 3 days, then secure the cake to the board. Trace the pattern, see page 148, onto greaseproof (parchment) paper. Scribe the ribbons, bells and bears on the cake top, then paint them with food colouring. Build up delicate colours lightly. Do not paint on one area for too long or you may dissolve the surface of the sugarpaste. Pipe the embroidery with pastel-coloured icing using a no. 0 piping tube (tip).

Pipe an outline around each bell using a no. 0 piping tube (tip). Attach three apple blossom flowers and two small cut-out butterflies to the cake with dots of icing. Make a point of telling the bride that sugar flowers containing stamens are not edible.

3 apple blossoms and 2 cut-out butterflies.

▼ Cut a strip of greaseproof (parchment) paper the same length and height as the side of the cake. Fold the pattern into six equal parts. Draw the garlands on each section taking care that all the pencil marks are kept to one side of the template. Place the pattern around the cake and scribe the line.
   Pipe the bulb border using a no. 3 piping tube (tip) and soft white icing – the bulbs must not touch. Overpipe the border with loops of pink icing using a no. 0 piping tube (tip).

▼ Begin piping the embroidery on the cake side and pipe the shapes of leaves. Paint the bows at the high point of each garland drape.

The motifs for the top design can be runout and painted separately if you are nervous about painting directly on the cake.

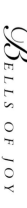

53

▲ Continue piping the garlands
of flowers in pastel colours
using a no. 0 piping tube (tip).
Pipe two small shells together
in the form of little hearts
among the flowers. Trim the
edge of the board with lace.

*The motifs for the top design can be
run out and painted separately if
you are nervous about painting
directly on the cake*

1.2m (1¼ yd) lace.

BE MINE FOR EVER

A beautifully embroidered, shell pink wedding gown,
inspired the design on this cake decorated with trellis
work and piped bells. Bunnies kissing
under a wedding arch make a
light-hearted top decoration to
contrast with the conservative royal icing design
– ideal for young lovers and the young at heart.

SKILLS
~
Trellis piping
Graduated line piping
Piped bells
Piped shells
Cut-out pastillage
Painting
Cut-out blossom

15cm (6 inch) square 6cm
(2½ inch) deep cake
20cm (8 inch) square 7.5cm
(3 inch) deep cake
15cm (6 inch) and 20cm
(8 inch) thin boards
18cm (7 inch) and 28cm
(11 inch) square boards
nos. 1 and 2 piping tubes (tips)
4 perspex pillars
perspex arch

Place the cakes on thin boards
of their exact size and cover
with marzipan (almond
paste). Make enough pale
pink royal icing to completely
coat the cakes and the boards.
  Cut a strip of paper to fit
around each cake. Fold the
paper into four to represent
one side, then fold one side
into four equal sections.
Draw the centre scallop and
two half scallops at each end.

Fold the paper in half
lengthways and trace the
scallop design for two sides.
Then cut out the pattern
double to cut the design in the
whole length of paper.

Cut a square of paper the size
of the cake top. Fold it into
quarters. Draw a curve to
correspond with the side
design. Repeat for each side.
Cut out the pattern.

Position the side pattern and pipe two rows of graduated line work along the top edge of the template. Turn the cake upside down and pipe the second set of line work using a no. 1 piping tube (tip).

▶ Cut a square of paper 1cm (½ inch) smaller than the board. Fold it into quarters, then draw the scallop pattern taking care to line up the points with the side design. Pipe two rows of graduated line work on the board around the template.

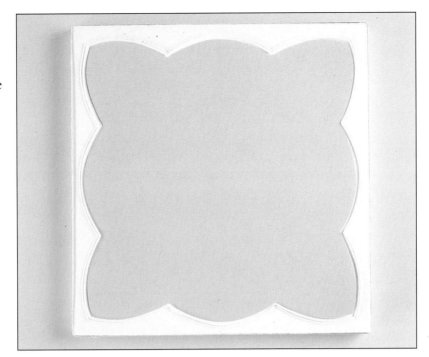

Get into the habit of drawing accurate templates and cutting them out with a scalpel for best results.

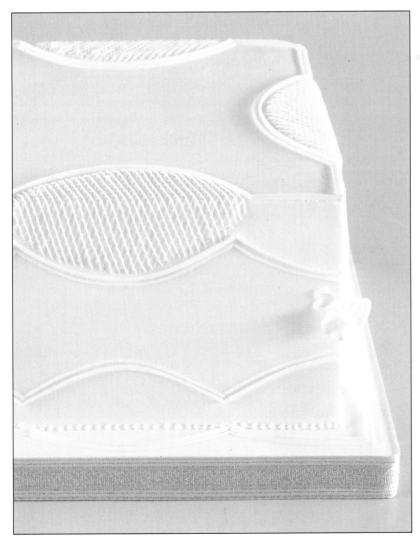

◀ Secure the cake to the board. Pipe a small shell border around the base using a no. 2 piping tube (tip). Pipe graduated line work around the top template. Pipe three rows of trellis work over the cake edge: the first straight, then the second two rows are piped at opposite diagonals. Trim the board edge.

2m (2¼ yd) × 1cm (½ inch) ribbon.

► The bells are piped onto wax paper using a no. 2 piping tube (tip). Pipe three bulbs of icing directly on top of each other. Allow to partially dry – the timing is crucial; when the outside of the bell is firm, scoop out the soft icing from inside with a cocktail stick (toothpick). Allow to dry.

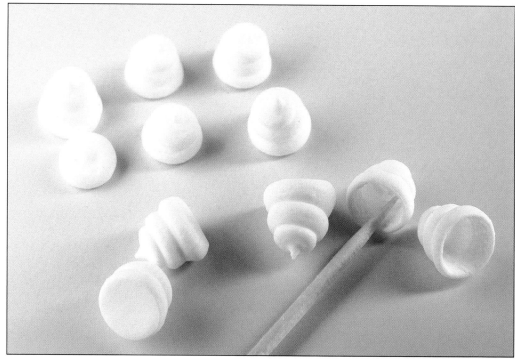

Pipe about 20 bells.

Pipe two heart shapes to form a bow on each corner of the cake. Attach the bells with a little royal icing. Pipe a line of royal icing and small dot inside each bell to represent the clanger.

◄ Using a scalpel cut out the bunny pieces, see page 147, from thinly rolled flower paste. Wire the blossoms into sprays. Paint the details on the bunnies with food colouring on the front and back. Stick the ears and arms to the body with royal icing. Place a small ball of flower paste on the perspex arch and arrange the blossom. Hang two piped bells from the arch centre.

Small amount of flower paste and 40 blossoms.

SWEET HEARTS

Fragile miniature roses and white frills are the classic combination for this special cake. Displayed on a velvet stand, five tiers of heart-shaped cakes make an eye-catching centrepiece for the wedding banquet.

<table>
<tr><td>

SKILLS
~
Cut-out frill
Piped embroidery
Herringbone piping
Moulded flowers

</td></tr>
</table>

15cm (6 inch) heart-shaped
5.5cm (2¼ inch) deep cake
two 20cm (8 inch) heart-
shaped 6cm (2½ inch) deep
cakes
two 25cm (10 inch) heart-
shaped 7.5cm (3 inch) deep
cakes
23cm (9 inch) and two 28cm
(11 inch) and 33cm (13 inch)
heart-shaped boards
no. 0 piping tube (tip)
pink velvet heart-shaped
cake stand

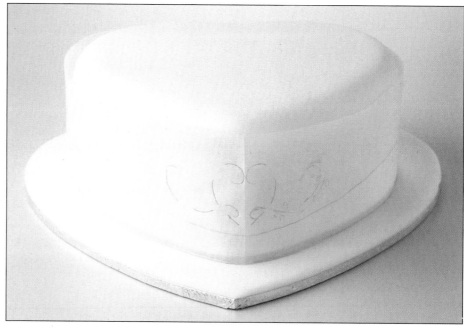

Coat the cakes with marzipan (almond paste) and white sugarpaste. Coat the boards with white sugarpaste and dry before fixing cakes in place.

▲ Cut a strip of greaseproof (parchment) paper the same height and length as the side of each cake. Fold the paper in half and mark a line, sloping down from the top of the heart at the back to 2.5cm (1 inch) from the bottom at the front point of the heart: this is the frill line. Trace the line onto the other side of the paper to match. Trace the embroidery, see page 147, on the heart point. Scribe the patterns on the cakes. Fix 3mm (⅛ inch) ribbon around cake bases with icing.

*About 9m (10 yd) ×
3mm (⅛ inch) wide pink
ribbon for cake bases*

► Position the first row of frills 5mm (¼ inch) below the scribe line, then place the second layer slightly above the line. Neaten the top edge of the frill by trimming it with a scalpel. Pipe a herringbone shell pattern above the frills using a no. 0 piping tube (tip).

◄ The embroidery is piped in white royal icing, using a no. 0 piping tube (tip). Trim the board edges with white and pink ribbon.

About 5m (5½ yd) × 5mm (¼ inch) wide each of white and pink ribbon for board edges.

If the velvet covering on the stand is marked, restore the pile by steaming it over a boiling kettle. Do not iron it.

▲ All the bouquets have a similar number of flowers but they are graduated in size. Wire the flowers into natural sprays, using smaller blooms for the smaller cakes.

Secure the bouquets to the cakes with a small piece of soft flower paste. Place a small ribbon bow over the flower stems in each bouquet.

About 100 rose leaves of assorted sizes, 120 Nazomi roses and buds with cotton centres, made using the pulled method of flower modelling and 6 small ribbon bows.

ST PAUL'S CHURCH

This outstanding cake will be a talking point at the reception. The cake can be personalized for the bride and groom by piping a plaque with the church name and a clock showing the time of the wedding ceremony. You may even wish to make bridesmaids dressed in the colour of the day.

SKILLS
~

Piped loops, lines and scrolls
Piped filigree
Cut-out pastillage
Cut-out blossoms

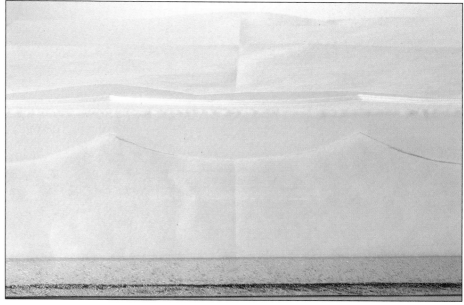

25cm (10 inch) square 6cm (2½ inch) deep cake
30 × 25cm (12 × 10 inch) and 38 × 33cm (15 × 13 inch) rectangular 7.5cm (3 inch) deep cakes
46 × 40cm (18 × 16 inch) rectangular board
nos. 2, 1.5, 0 and 42 piping tubes (tip)

Place rectangular cakes on thin boards of same size. Coat with marzipan (almond paste) and royal icing. Secure large cake to board. Fill any gaps with icing.

▲ Cut templates for both cakes. Cut a piece of greaseproof (parchment) paper the same size as the top of the cake. Divide each side into three, fold the paper into quarters and draw the pattern. Cut out the template. Cut a side template, matching the scallop points on the side and top.
Place the template on the cake top and pipe an outline using a no. 2 piping tube (tip). Secure side template around the cake; outline with a no. 2 piping tube. Remove the template. Use a no. 1.5 piping tube to overpipe two lines.

Pipe the filigree work over top edge using a no. 0 piping tube (tip).

Place the middle tier on the bottom tier and fill in any gaps around the upper cake with royal icing.

▶ Using a no. 1.5 piping tube (tip) pipe drop loops evenly spaced 1cm (½ inch) from the base of each cake. Follow the loops as a piping guide and use a no. 42 piping tube (tip) to pipe the rope design just below them. Overpipe the rope using a no. 1.5 piping tube (tip). Attach three cut-out blossoms over each scallop. Pipe small shells using a no. 1.5 piping tube (tip) to represent leaves. Three different-sized blossoms are positioned at each corner.

About 75 cut-out blossoms.

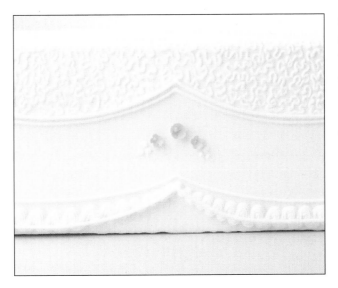

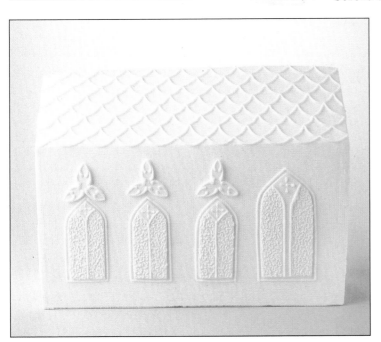

▼ Cut the cake for the church and assemble it following the diagram, see page 149, using apricot purée to stick the pieces together. Place on a thin board cut to the exact size of the cake. Coat the two ends with marzipan, then coat the front, both sides of the roof and the back with one piece of marzipan. Coat the cake with royal icing, allowing each flat side to dry before coating an adjacent

side. This may be time consuming but it will ensure that all the edges are sharp and neat.

Cut the pastillage pieces using cardboard templates, see page 149, and a scalpel to ensure they are all accurate. Follow the numbering on the templates for the number of sections required. Place them on a flat surface to dry. Pipe the details illustrated on the window templates, using a no. 0 piping tube (tip) for the filigree work, and a no. 2 piping tube (tip) for the lines.

About 1kg (2 lb) pastillage.

▼ Pipe drop loops on the top using a no. 2 piping tube (tip) to resemble a tiled roof. Then attach the piped windows to the sides of the cake with a little royal icing.

▶ Use fine sandpaper to remove any excess sugar from the dried pastillage pieces. Pipe two lines on top of each other, 5mm (¼ inch) from the top of each of the four tower pieces. Leave to dry, then assemble the pieces, using royal icing to hold them together. The join lines should not show on the front of the tower. Leave to dry flat.

Place the eight spire pieces, right sides down, together on sponge/foam arranging them with points together and sides touching, see diagram on page 143. Roll out a thin circle of pastillage, brush it liberally with egg white and lay it over the spire pieces. Gently rub the back of the pastillage to stick it securely, then trim off excess paste around the outer edge of the spire pieces. Carefully pick up the pieces and shape them into an octagonal spire. The pastillage backing on the pieces strengthens the spire and ensures that the joins are neatly filled. Allow to dry.

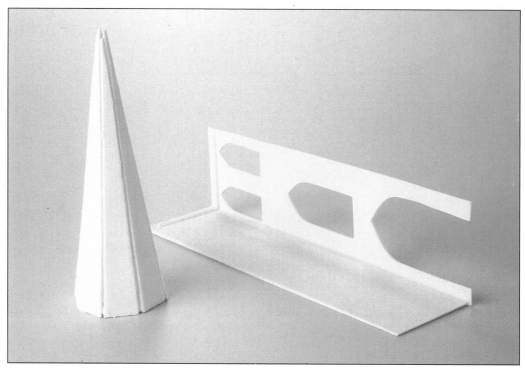

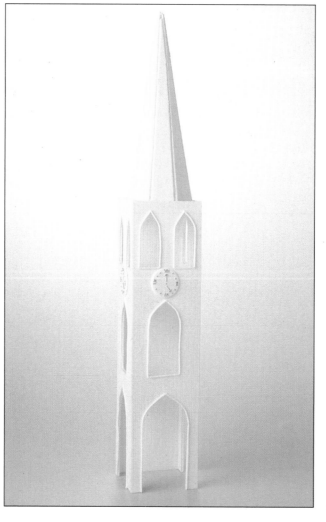

◀ Using a no. 2 piping tube (tip) pipe around the tower windows and arches. Pipe the clock details with a no. 0 piping tube (tip) and paint with gold food colouring. Attach the clocks to the tower with a little royal icing.

◀ Fix the roof support in the top of the tower resting it on the piped lines of icing and using dots of icing to secure it in place. When dry the spire can be positioned carefully on top of the tower.

To assemble the church, place the cake on the top tier. Position the tower. Hold the large and small window panels in place with pieces of sponge/foam. Use royal icing to secure the roof pieces. When dry remove the sponge and position cornice pieces on each corner of the cake.

ROSES *for* SUSAN

Life-like sprays of roses complete with raindrops lead
the eye down this three-tier cake – a traditional
design based on the
classic themes of
flowers and beautiful
embroidered bridal gowns.

15 × 10cm (6 × 4 inch),
20 × 15cm (8 × 6 inch) and
25 × 20cm (10 × 8 inch)
oval cakes
23 × 18cm (9 × 7 inch),
28 × 23cm (11 × 9 inch) and
33 × 28cm (13 × 11 inch)
oval boards
nos. 1, 0 and 00 piping
tubes (tips)
perspex celtube, made to
measure for cake stand

Draw around the tins (pans)
used to bake the cakes on a
sheet of paper. Reposition the
tins to cover a small portion
of the edge and draw a
matching arc on each oval.
Cut out the templates and use
to cut the cakes to shape.
Reserve the templates for the
top piping.
Coat the cakes with marzipan
(almond paste); leave to dry.

Cover the cakes and boards
separately with white
sugarpaste. Allow to dry for
3 days. Secure the coated
cakes to the boards. Secure
3mm (⅛ inch) wide ribbon
around the base of each cake
with royal icing.

4.5m (5 yd) × 3mm
(⅛ inch) ribbon.

Measure the height and circumference of each cake, excluding the curved front. Make a greaseproof (parchment) paper template for each cake. Fold the paper into six equal sections. Measure one section, divide it into three and mark dots 5mm (¼ inch) from the bottom edge. Repeat for other sections. Draw a scallop line for the top of the extension work, see page 150. Trace the embroidery design on each section of the template, ensuring all pencil lines are kept to one side of paper only. Pin the templates to the cakes and scribe through the paper.

◄ Brush embroidery is used for the larger petals. Use a no. 1 piping tube (tip) and white royal icing to pipe brush embroidered petals, brushing each one with a damp paint brush as it is piped. Using the same tube, pipe the remaining petals with a zig-zag action. Complete the embroidery with drop loops and line-piped stems.

▲ The extension work is supported by a loop of icing, see page 101. Place pins in the scribe marks. Brush the pins with a little vegetable fat. Using a no. 1 piping tube (tip) drop a loop from the cake front over the pins, the loop must not touch the board. Pipe the extension work with a no. 00 piping tube (tip). Then carefully remove the pins. Pipe another loop of icing over the bottom edge of extension work to neaten it.

Attach the lace above the extension work with dots of icing. If this extension work, supported on a loop, is too delicate or advanced, a bridge can be piped or this border omitted. Place the prepared template on the cake top. Use a no. 0 piping tube (tip) and white royal icing to outline the template with small 'S' and 'C' scrolls.

Pipe 300 lace pieces, see page 150, using a no. 0 piping tube (tip).

▲ To make the flower sprays, wire the roses and leaves into two returns (or two sections) and bind them together at the centre point. Insert a posy holder into the front of each cake. Place a small piece of flower paste inside each holder so that as the flowers are put into place the paste sets and holds them firmly in position. Trim the boards with ribbon.

2.6m (3 yd) × 5mm (¼ inch) picot edge ribbon. Make 30 roses at different stages of development and 70 rose leaves of assorted sizes.

When making the arrangements of sugar flowers on this cake, to achieve the most realistic effect, I used sprays of fresh flowers as models, even down to sprinkling water on the flowers to resemble dew drops.

BLUEBIRDS *of* LOVE

A novel single tier design made up of
two layers of cake to achieve
the depth. The side panels,
which stand proud of the cake,
frame the wedding bell decoration.

SKILLS
~
Runout collars
Brush embroidery
Piped dots
Figure piping
Line piping

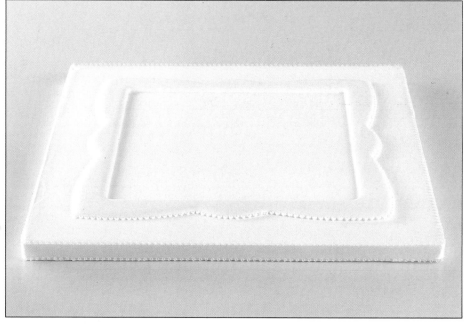

two 15cm (6 inch) square
7.5cm (3 inch) deep cakes
30cm (12 inch) square board
two 15cm (6 inch) square thin
boards
nos. 1 and 2 piping tubes (tips)

Trim the cakes to exactly
7.5cm (3 inch) deep. Place the
cakes on thin boards cut to
their exact size, then coat
them with marzipan (almond
paste). Place one cake on top
of the other, leaving the board
between the layers. Coat the
cake and board with salmon
pink royal icing. Allow each
side to dry before coating the
next to obtain neat edges.

▲ Make the runout collars,
see page 151 and leave to dry
under a warm lamp. When
the collars are dry, pipe a
picot edge using a no. 1
piping tube on the inside edge
of both sets of side panels; on
the inside and outside edges
of the top collar; on the
outside edge of the base
collar; and on the top of the
flange pieces. Leave to dry.

► Secure the board collar in place with softened icing. Secure the coated cake to the board with icing taking care to keep an even space all around between the collar and cake.

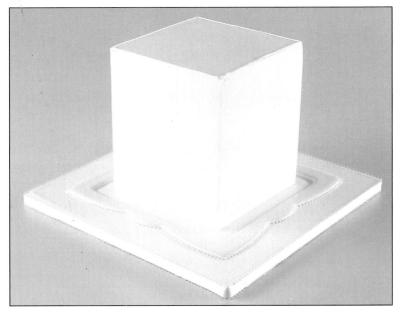

◄ Pipe the design on the bells using a deeper shade of salmon pink icing and a no. 1 piping tube (tip). When the icing is dry attach the bells to the cake sides. Scribe the ribbon design above the bells on the cake, then pressure pipe the ribbon with soft peak royal icing. Attach the birds.

◄ Carefully trace the flower design, see page 152, on the side panel. Use a no. 1 piping tube (tip), a deeper shade of salmon pink royal icing and leaf green royal icing to brush embroider the side panels, then allow to dry. Pipe softened icing on the brush-embroidered side panel and attach the plain front side panel on top around the edge making sure the two pieces are exactly in line. Allow to dry completely.

◀ Attach the top base collar to the cake using a no. 2 piping tube (tip) and softened icing. Pipe icing along the top edge of the top base collar and along the bottom edge of the side panel. Then carefully position the side panel, clean excess icing away immediately using a clean soft brush. Repeat with the remaining side panels.

▶ Using a no. 2 piping tube (tip), pipe a line on the top of the cake around the collar. Pipe some soft icing on the collar edge and attach the upper collar.

When cut, the separate cake layers provide twice the portions obtained from a single 15cm (6 inch) cake.

◀ Arrange the flange pieces on graph paper and secure them together at the corners with royal icing. Use the graph paper to fix the flanges in a perfect square. Allow to dry, then attach to the top collar with royal icing. Trim the board edge with ribbon.

1.2m (1¼ yd) × 1cm (½ inch) ribbon.

WITH MY LOVE

The clean lines of this formal
design are softened and enhanced
by a subtle pattern of stencilled hearts
applied to the cake sides and lace
pieces on the cake edges.

SKILLS
~
*Cut-out pastillage
collars
Lace
Stencilling
Graduated line piping
Moulded flowers*

13cm (5 inch) hexagonal
5.5cm (2¼ inch) deep cake
18cm (7 inch) hexagonal 6cm
(2½ inch) deep cake
23cm (9 inch) hexagonal
7.5cm (3 inch) deep cake
20cm (8 inch), 25cm (10 inch)
and 33cm (13 inch) hexagonal
boards
small metal stencil for side
design
nos. 1, 2 and 0 piping
tubes (tips)
porcelain bride and groom
6 round chalk or plaster
cake pillars

▶ Coat the cakes with
marzipan (almond paste) as
if coating with royal icing.
Coat the boards and cake
tops with white sugarpaste.
Allow to dry for 3 days. Roll
out long strips of sugarpaste
and apply to the sides of the
cakes. Join the paste neatly at
the back. Secure the cakes to
the boards. Allow the coating
to dry.

◀ It is worth covering the
board edge with paper when
applying the stencil design to
protect it from colour
spillage. Use a small metal
stencil and a flat-end stencil
brush to gently work green
dusting powder (petal dust/
blossom tint) through the
pattern onto the cake.

▶ A different design can be used for each tier or the same one may be applied to the whole cake. An alphabet stencil and pink colouring was used for the 'K' on the bottom tier. Cut out a hexagonal template 1cm (½ inch) smaller than the top of the coated cake. Use a no. 1 piping tube (tip) to pipe three rows of graduated line work. Pipe the inside lines using green royal icing.

◀ Using the pattern on page 153, cut six collar pieces in finely rolled pastillage for each tier. Dry flat. Place the collar pattern on the board and pipe three rows of graduated line work with green outside lines.

750g (1½ lb) pastillage.

◀ Use a no. 2 piping tube (tip) to pipe a shell border around the base of each cake. Trim the board edges with white lace. Attach the collar pieces to the cake using softened royal icing. Dry.
   Pipe one hundred and fifty lace pieces, see page 153, using a no. 0 piping tube. Dry. Secure to outer collar edge with dots of royal icing.

3.4m (3¾ yd) lace.

WITH MY LOVE

► Pipe a bulb of royal icing on each of the corners of the cakes in turn and assemble the miniature bouquets of flowers. These are made up of three pulled flowers and a fern leaf with sprays of blossom.

Make 60 sprays of blossom, 60 pulled flowers with long stamens and 20 fern leaves.

◄ For the gazebo top piece, cut out six side panels from finely rolled pastillage, see page 153. Dry flat. Lay the side panels in line on sponge/foam butting them close together. Roll out thin strips of pastillage, dampen them with water and use to tape together the joins between the pastillage pieces. Stand the gazebo up and bend into shape. Support until dry. Place the roof pieces on the sponge with their points together and all but two sides touching. Roll out a piece of pastillage thinly, dampen with water and lay it over the roof pieces to cover them. Cut away the excess paste with a scalpel. Bend the roof into its hexagonal shape. Dry. Position the gazebo sides and the roof over the bride and groom on the cake. Pipe small shells down each side panel and lines on the roof using a no. 1 piping tube. Attach the lace pieces to the roof edge.

SYMBOL *of* HAPPINESS

Sugared almonds nestle into the sprays
of silk flowers on this stunning cake.
The almonds, symbolizing health,
wealth, happiness, fertility and long
life, are distributed among the
guests at Greek and Italian weddings.

SKILLS
~
*Piped dots for
embroidery*

13cm (5 inch) round 6cm
(2½ inch) deep cake
23cm (9 inch) trefoil-shaped
7.5cm (3 inch) deep cake
30cm (12 inch) round 7.5cm
(3 inch) deep cake
13cm (5 inch) and 30cm
(12 inch) round thin boards
23cm (9 inch) thin trefoil
board
18cm (7 inch) and 38cm
(15 inch) round boards
no. 1 piping tube (tip)
Colonnade separator

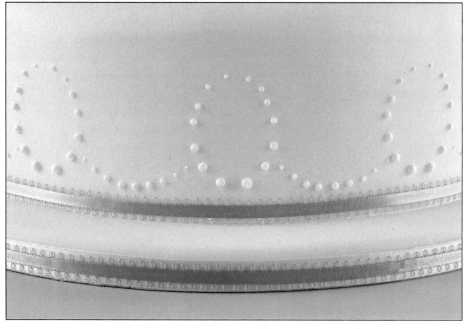

▲ Cut thin boards to the
exact sizes of the cakes. Coat
the cakes with marzipan
(almond paste) and white
sugarpaste. Allow to dry for
3 days. Secure the top and
bottom tiers to the coated
boards. Place the middle tier
directly on the bottom tier.
Cut a strip of paper the same
length and height as the cake
sides. Fold the top-tier
template into six sections, the
middle-tier template into
three sections and the
bottom-tier template into
twelve sections. Draw the
design on page 153 on every
section of the pattern,
adjusting it to fit as necessary.
Place the templates around
the cakes and make a pin hole
for each dot. Remove the
patterns.

Attach 5mm (¼ inch) ribbon around the base of each cake with royal icing. Trim the edge of the boards with ribbon. Use a no. 1 piping tube (tip) and soft royal icing to pipe the embroidery, making dots of different sizes, see left.

4.5m (5 yd) × 5mm (¼ inch) ribbon.

▶ Enclose the sugared almonds in the net leaves of the sprays of flowers. Attach three sprays to the middle tier with royal icing.

7 sprays of silk flowers with net leaves and pearl sprays.

◀ Make the top decoration from the silk flowers, net leaves and almonds. Assemble the stems in a piece of sugarpaste and build up the arrangement from all sides. As a finishing touch, a spray of flowers is taped to the handle of the knife which is to be used at the cake-cutting ceremony.

REGAL TRADITIONS

Pure white icing and silver horseshoes
complement the bold piping and
symmetric design on this
beautiful, traditional wedding cake
to mark a classic occasion.

SKILLS

Scrolls
Graduated line piping
Piped shells
Template preparation
Moulded flowers

13cm (5 inch) round 6cm
(2½ inch) deep cake
20cm (8 inch) round 7.5cm
(3 inch) deep cake
28cm (11 inch) round 10cm
(4 inch) deep cake
13cm (5 inch), 20cm (8 inch)
and 28cm (11 inch) round
thin boards
20cm (8 inch), 28cm (11 inch)
and 38cm (15 inch) round
boards
no. 1 piping tube (tip)
7 perspex candy-twist cake
pillars

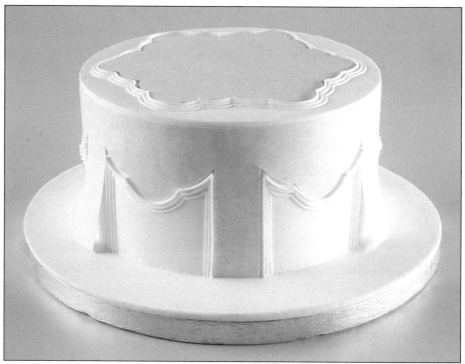

▲ Place the cakes on thin
boards of their exact sizes.
Coat with marzipan (almond
paste). Coat the boards and
cakes with royal icing. Secure
the cakes to the boards and
fill in any gaps with icing.

Cut a template the same
length and height of the side
of each cake. Cut circles of
paper the same size as the
cake tops. Fold the circles
into six equal sections, draw
and cut out the scallop
pattern, see page 153. Fold
the side template into six and
cut out the side design, see
page 153, adjusting the size
for each tier. Position the
templates, lining up the top
and side designs. Using a no.
1 piping tube (tip), pipe
graduated line work around
the top and side templates.

Tilt the cake away from you. Using a no. 1 piping tube (tip), pipe five rows of graduated line work over the top edge between each side panel.

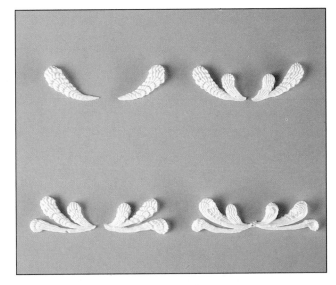

▶ Pipe the scrolls around the top edge of the cake using a no. 42 piping tube (tip), following the step-by-step picture. Then overpipe the scrolls using a no. 2 piping tube (tip).

◀ Use a no. 42 piping tube (tip) to pipe shells around the cake base between each panel. Overpipe as illustrated using a no. 2 piping tube (tip). Attach the horseshoes to the cakes with royal icing. Trim the board edges with ribbon.

6 each of large, medium and small silver horse-shoes and 3m (3¼ yd) patterned ribbon.

▶ Place a piece of flower paste on a pillar. Arrange the flowers and pearl loops, building up the arrangement to a point. Leave to set.

10 white sugar roses, 10 peach pulled flowers and buds, 8 bouvardia, 16 rose leaves, 7 eucalyptus leaves, 6 miniature arum lilies and 9 sprays of pearl loops.

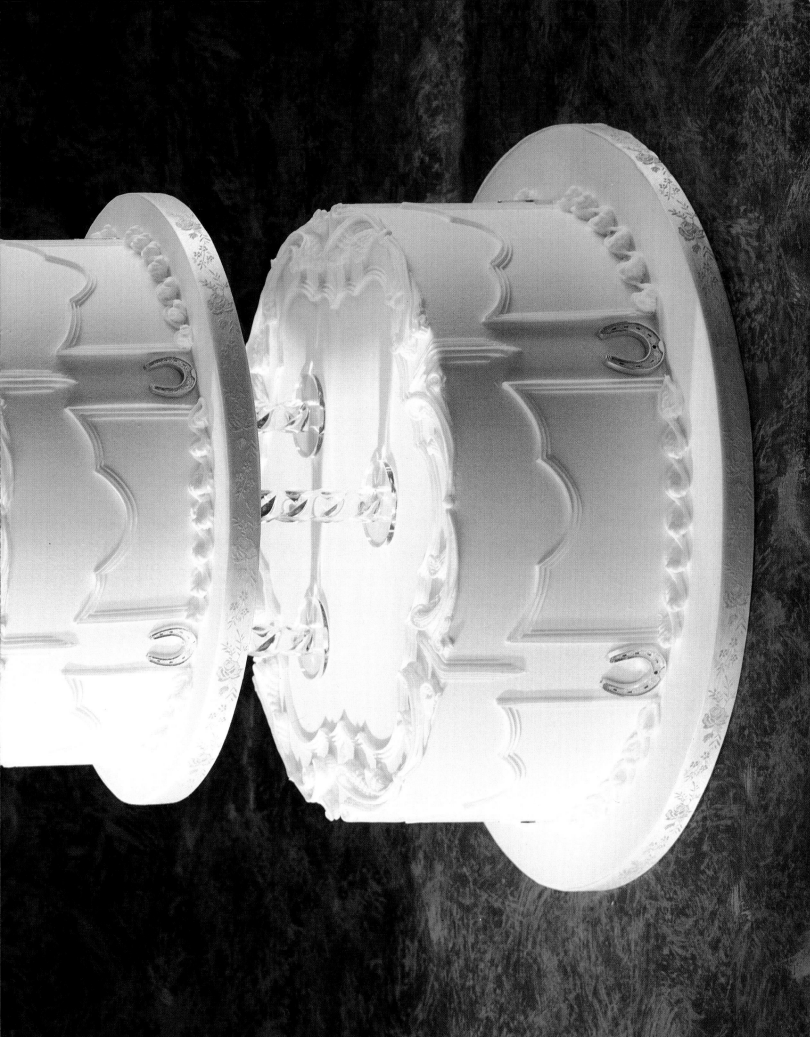

FAIRYTALE WEDDING

For the bride who plans a fairytale
wedding, this sparkling, ten-tier cake
will make an unforgetable centrepiece
at the celebration breakfast. The illuminated water
fountain complements the arrangement without
detracting from the cakes.

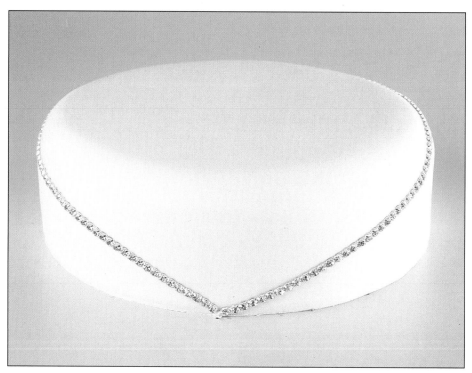

two 10cm (4 inch) round 5cm
(2 inch) deep cakes
two 14cm (5½ inch) round
5.5cm (2¼ inch) deep cakes
two 16.5cm (6¾ inch) round
6mm (2½ inch) deep cakes
two 20cm (8 inch) round
6.5cm (2¾ inch) deep cakes
two 23cm (9 inch) round
7.5cm (3 inch) deep cakes
two 16cm (6½ inch), 20cm
(8 inch), 23.5cm (9¼ inch),
26cm (10½ inch) and 29cm
(11½ inch) round boards
no. 1 piping tube (tip)
right and left five-tier perspex
stands
electric illuminated water
fountain

▲ The sizes of the cakes and
boards must be accurate to fit
on the stand. Trim the cakes
to the correct depth and cover
them with marzipan (almond
paste). Coat one cake at a
time with cream (celebration)
sugarpaste. Attach the
diamanté while the coating is
soft: brush egg white on the
back of the string of
diamanté. Then, beginning at
the centre back of the cake,
bring the diamanté down
both sides of the cake to meet
at the front. Push slightly
with a smoother to embed the
back of the diamanté in the
paste. Take great care as the
coating will mark easily when

touched. Coat the boards with sugarpaste and allow to dry for 3 days. Trim the board edges with ribbon.

7.2m (8 yd) diamanté and 8.6m (9½ yd) × 5mm (¼ inch) picot edge ribbon.

▶ Attach the cakes to the boards. Use a no. 0 piping tube (tip) and cream icing, pipe the filigree work around the sides of the cakes. Pipe a picot edge around the base of each cake using a no. 1 piping tube (tip).

▲ Make ten bouquets of flowers for the cakes and one larger one for the stand. Secure them to the cakes with softened flower paste. Use a hat pin to support the flowers until the paste has set.

Make 30 lilies, 15 lily buds, 70 sprays of white blossom dusted with pink and blue dusting powder (petal dust/ blossom tint) and 100 sprays of wired gypsophila.

Always remind the bride about any inedible decorations used on a cake, such as the diamanté trimming in this case.

▲ The large bouquet of lilies is taped to a perspex stand, of the type sold in craft shops to support porcelain dolls.

The self-contained fountain is pumped by electric. Liquid food colouring has been added to tint the water pale pink.

BOUQUET CASCADE

A modern design for a traditional three-tier cake. A cut-out section in each cake holds a bouquet of sugar flowers which gracefully cascade down to the tier below. The hand-painted border completes the decoration on a cake which is eye-catching from all angles.

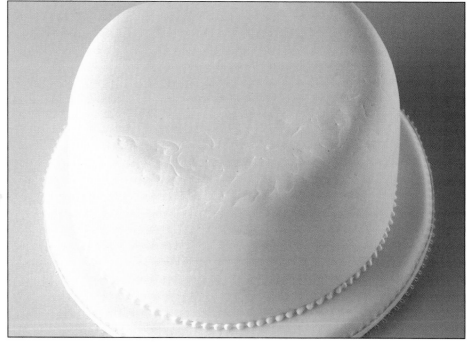

SKILLS
~
Fat painting
Piped shells
Line piping
Moulded flowers

13cm (5 inch) round 5cm
(2 inch) deep cake
20cm (8 inch) round 6cm
(2½ inch) deep cake
25cm (10 inch) round 7.5cm
(3 inch) deep cake
19cm (7½ inch), 28cm
(11 inch) and 36cm (14 inch)
round boards
3 posy holders
nos. 2 and 0 piping tubes (tips)
high staggered stand

▲ Cut a small curved section out of each cake. Coat the cakes with marzipan (almond paste). Coat the cakes and boards with champagne-coloured sugarpaste. Insert the posy holders into the sides of the curved sections while the sugarpaste is soft; dry. Secure cakes to boards with a little royal icing. Make a paper template, see page 155. Fold the paper in half to find the centre back and begin tracing the design onto the cake from this point. Scribe the pattern from the cake top down the sides. Take care to ensure that the pattern does not slip. Pipe a shell border around the cake base using a no. 2 piping tube (tip).

► Melt a little white vegetable fat (shortening) or cocoa butter on a plate over boiling water. Mix dusting power (petal dust/blossom tint) of the required colour with a little of the fat, then paint the roses, leaves and blossom with a very light shade of the colours. Take care not to touch the painting as the colours do not set quickly and they may smudge.

▼ Gradually paint in more detail by brushing on cream, brown, yellow and pink. To produce very deep colours, keep the fat hot and mix in the dusting powder (petal dust/blossom tint) to produce a paste consistency.

► Use a no. 0 piping tube (tip) to pipe a thin line of white royal icing around the edge of some leaves and petals. Trim the boards with cream ribbon.

About 2.6m (3 yd) × 5mm (¼ inch) picot ribbon.

◄ Wire the flowers into three shower bouquets, each made up of an open rose, two closed roses, filler flowers and gypsophila. Add three ribbon loops to each bouquet. Transport the flowers separately; the wire stem of the bouquets will sit firmly in the posy holders, and may be positioned once the cake is assembled.

6 closed roses, 3 open roses and about 100 assorted filler flowers. Wire small sprays of dried gypsophila together and make 9 ribbon loops from 1.4m (1½ yd) × 3mm (⅛ inch) ribbon.

DREAM MAKER

The traditional round wedding
cake symbolizes a circle without
a beginning and no end – eternity.
The top decoration of a ring in a
silver shell continues the eternity theme
and it can be treasured as a wedding-day keepsake.

SKILLS
~
Crimping
Piped shells
Piped roses
Cut-out frill
Ribbon insertion

15cm (6 inch) round 5.5cm
(2¼ inch) deep cake
20cm (8 inch) round 6cm
(2½ inch) deep cake
26cm (10 inch) round 7.5cm
(3 inch) deep cake
23cm (9 inch), 28cm (11 inch)
and 36cm (14 inch) round
boards
scallop crimper
round frill cutter
no. 1 piping tube (tip)
silver shell stand for top
decoration
costume jewellery ring
'E' cake stand

▲ Coat the cakes with
marzipan (almond paste).
Coat the boards with pink
sugarpaste and allow to dry.
Decorate each tier separately.
Coat the cake with white
sugarpaste. Cut a strip of
paper the same height and
length as the side of the cake.
Fold the paper in half
lengthways, open it out, then
fold it into six equal portions
widthways. Cut the scallop

design, see page 155, into the
folded paper, adjusting it
slightly, if necessary, to fit
your cake. Pin the pattern
around the cake, centred on
the height.

Crimp the design in the
sugarpaste while the coating
is still soft. Allow the coating
to dry for 3 days before
placing the cake on the
prepared cake boards.

▼ Use a round frill cutter to make the sugarpaste frill. Dampen the board and position the frill. Pipe a shell border using a no. 1 tube (tip) around the cake base on top of the frill to conceal the join.

▼ Cut a circle of greaseproof (parchment) paper 7.5cm (3 inches) smaller than the top of the cake top. Fold the circle into six equal sections, then mark and cut a trefoil shape. Place the pattern on the cake and use it as a guide for the three curves of ribbon insertion, leaving spaces for flowers. Take care to align the template with the side design.

▲ Secure the piped roses to the top and side of the cake with dots of royal icing. Pipe small green shells using a no. 1 piping tube (tip) to represent leaves. Trim the board edge with picot ribbon.

81 piped pink roses and 2.6m (3 yd) × 5mm (¼ inch) white picot ribbon.

◀ For the ring case top decoration, make a cushion of pink sugarpaste inside the shell and insert a costume jewellery ring. Place a small piece of sugarpaste at the back of the ring shell and insert the ribbon loops and wired piped roses to form a neat arrangement.

About 7 ribbon loops made from 2.6m (3 yd) lurex ribbon and 24 piped roses on wires.

FORGET-ME-NOT

The delightful little sugar bride and groom sitting
on a merry-go-round horse
make an unusual top piece
on this graceful design.

SKILLS
~

*Double bridgeless
extension work
Runout figures and
models
Painting
Lace
Moulded flowers*

18 × 13cm (7 × 5 inch) oval
6cm (2½ inch) deep cake
25 × 20cm (10 × 8 inch) oval
7.5cm (3 inch) deep cake
25 × 20cm (10 × 8 inch) and
36 × 30cm (14 × 12 inch) oval
boards
nos. 0, 00 and 1 piping tubes
(tips)
perspex barley-twist oval
divider

Coat the cakes with marzipan (almond paste) and white sugarpaste. Coat the boards with sugarpaste. Allow to dry for 3 days. Secure the cakes to the boards. Attach 3mm (⅛ inch) wide ribbon around the base of each cake. Use a no. 0 piping tube (tip) and softened royal icing to pipe a picot edge on the board around the cake base. Trim the board edge with ribbon.

2.2m (2½ yd) × 5mm (¼ inch) wide picot edge ribbon.

▲ Cut oval templates the size of the cake tops. Trace the pattern, see page 154, then scribe the flowers and guidelines for the lace. Paint the roses and leaves with food colouring. Cut templates the same height and length as each cake side. Fold the templates into eight equal sections. Mark the bottom edge of the section into three and draw in the top concave curved line and the scallop bridge line, see page 154. Trace the pattern onto each section of the template. Scribe the design through the paper template onto the cake side.

► Insert pins in groups of four for the lower extension work between the rose sprays. Grease the pins with white vegetable fat (shortening). Pipe a loop of icing over the pins using a no. 1 piping tube (tip). Allow to dry. Pipe the extension work from the scribed line to the piped loop using a no. 00 piping tube (tip).

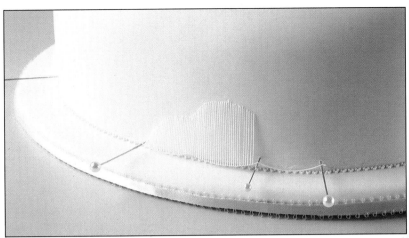

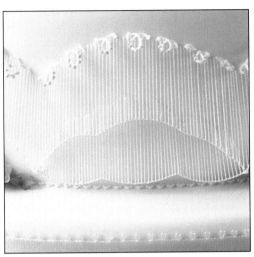

◄ Insert the pins for the second layer of extension work. Protect the top of the cake with clean paper, then turn the cake upside down. Use a no. 1 piping tube (tip) to pipe loops of royal icing over the greased pins – the loops should touch the corners of the first bridge line as this helps to support the icing. Allow to dry. Turn the cake over.

This exhibition-style cake highlights several skills – painted garlands of roses, piped lace and delicate sprays of roses and forget-me-nots that are nestled in the extension work.

► Place four small pea-sized pieces of sugarpaste on the board between the lower sections of extension work. Using tweezers, carefully assemble the flower sprays. Pipe the second row of extension work using a no. 00 piping tube (tip).

Make 50 roses and buds, 32 sprays of forget-me-nots and 50 tiny rose leaves.

Using a no. 00 piping tube (tip), pipe three hundred and fifty lace pieces on non-stick paper, see page 154. Attach the lace above the extension work.

▶ Attach the perspex cake divider to the bottom tier with dots of royal icing to prevent the divider moving. Position two rows of lace on the cake top. Placing the divider first avoids damaging the lace.

◀ Make the runout pieces for the top piece, see page 154 and dry. Turn the bride and groom bodies over and run-out their backs. Paint the details on the runouts with food colouring.

Secure the horse's body pieces together at the top edge with royal icing and allow to dry. Then, lay the body on the edge of a 1cm (½ inch) piece of sponge/foam and attach the bride and groom, the head, ear and tail with royal icing. Attach the bride's and groom's legs which will cover the joins and any noticeable icing. When dry, carefully turn the horse over and secure the second arms, legs and ears.

Use dots of icing to attach small cut-out blossoms to the bride's head and horse's neck.

WEDGWOOD BLUE

Delicate embroidery
and figure piping in white
on pale blue are characteristic of
the Wedgwood-style decoration on this
classic, timeless design.

SKILLS
~

Figure piping
Hollow stem piping
Graduated line piping
Miniature scroll piping

13cm (5 inch) octagonal 5.5cm
(2¼ inch) deep cake
18cm (7 inch) octagonal 6cm
(2½ inch) deep cake
23cm (9 inch) octagonal 7.5cm
(3 inch) deep cake
13cm (5 inch), 18cm (7 inch)
and 23cm (9 inch) octagonal
thin boards
20cm (8 inch), 25cm (10 inch)
and 30cm (12 inch) octagonal
boards
nos. 2 and 1 piping tubes (tips)
Celtiers stand

▶ Place the cakes on thin
boards cut to their exact size.
Cover with marzipan (almond
paste). Coat the boards and
cakes with Wedgwood blue
royal icing.

▶ Cut octagonal templates
1cm (½ inch) smaller than the
tops of the cakes. Draw the
two inner hexagonal shapes
and the embroidery design,
see page 155.
Position a template on one
cake and scribe only the
embroidery lines. Pipe a line
around the template and the
cake edge using a no. 2 piping
tube (tip). Remove the template.
Cut out the centre octagonal
and replace the template. Pipe
a line on the inside edge of
the paper. Repeat for the
second octagonal.

▶ Pipe one line on the board
next to the cake and another
1cm (½ inch) away. Using a
no. 1 piping tube (tip), pipe
small scrolls between the line
borders on the cake top and
board.

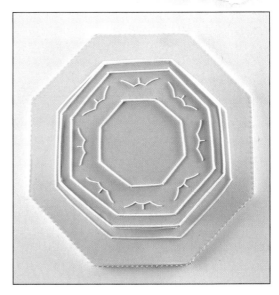

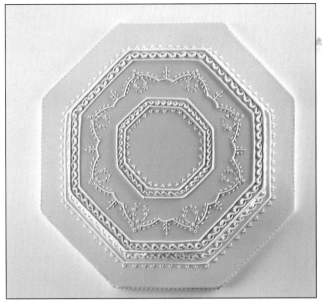

► Pipe the embroidery over the scribed lines using a no. 1 piping tube (tip). Pipe two small shells together to form a heart and repeat around the inside edge of the smallest piped octagonal and around the outside line on the board.

► Cut a paper template to fit one side panel. Draw the hollow stem design and a dot for the centre of each flower, see page 155. Scribe the design on each cake panel. Pipe the hollow stem designs on the side panels following the step-by-step stages shown. Reduce the drawing of the design for the smaller tiers.

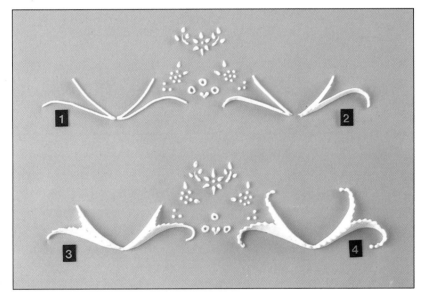

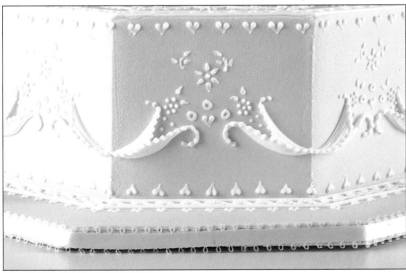

◄ Pipe shell hearts around the top and bottom edges of the cake sides. Trim the board edges with ribbon.

3.2m (3½ yd) × 5mm (¼ inch) picot edge ribbon.

WEDGWOOD BLUE

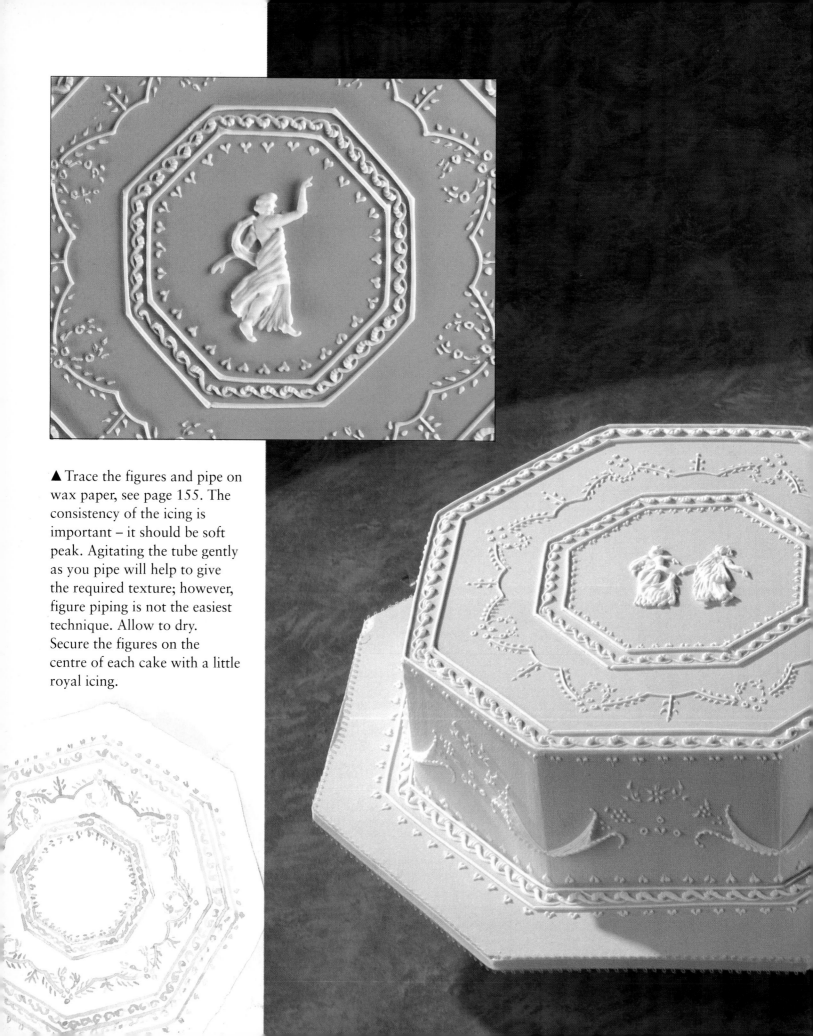

▲ Trace the figures and pipe on wax paper, see page 155. The consistency of the icing is important – it should be soft peak. Agitating the tube gently as you pipe will help to give the required texture; however, figure piping is not the easiest technique. Allow to dry. Secure the figures on the centre of each cake with a little royal icing.

SPRING WEDDING

The delicate colour and bold arrangements of
sugar daisies perfectly balance the geometric
design for the extension work on this fresh cake
which has particular appeal for spring brides.

SKILLS
~

*Cut-out pastillage
Diagonal extension
work
Stencilling
Piped shells
Moulded flowers*

15cm (6 inch) square 6cm
(2½ inch) deep cake
23cm (9 inch) square 6.5cm
(2¾ inch) deep cake
30cm (12 inch) square 7.5cm
(3 inch) deep cake
23cm (9 inch), 30cm (12 inch)
and 38cm (15 inch) square
boards
nos. 2 and 1 piping tubes (tips)
8 barley-twist perspex pillars
perspex stand for top piece

▲ Cover the cakes with
marzipan (almond paste) and
white sugarpaste. Coat the
boards. Dry for 3 days. Secure
the cakes to the boards.

Make a stencil, see page
156, long enough to complete
one side of the cake. Place the
stencil on the top of the cake,
ensuring it is straight. Spread
lemon-coloured royal icing
over the stencil using a
cranked pallet knife. Lift the
stencil away from one end.
Leave to dry. Clean the stencil
with a damp cloth. Stencil the
remaining two sides to form a
square. Stencil all the cakes,
adjusting the length of the
stencils to fit.

► Repeat the stencilling technique on the sides of the cakes. Using cardboard templates, see page 156, cut out fifty triangles of each size from thinly rolled pastillage. Pipe a shell border around the base of the cake using a no. 2 piping tube (tip). Measure the side of the cake and mark equal divisions about 2.5cm (1 inch) apart. Secure the triangles to the cake with lines of royal icing piped using a no. 1 piping tube (tip). Trim the edge of the board with ribbon.

About 60g (2 oz) pastillage and 3.6m (4 yd) × 5mm (¼ inch) ribbon.

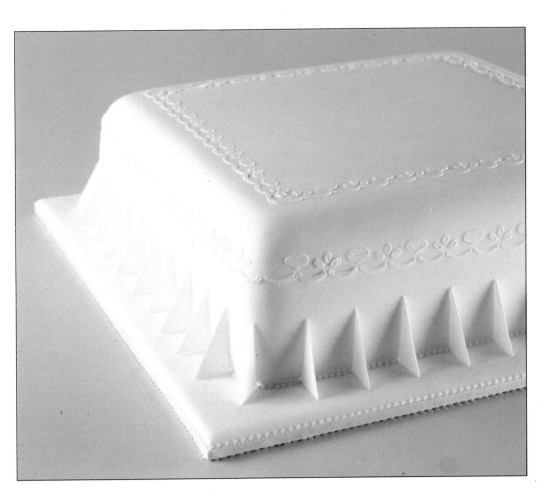

◄ Using a no. 1 piping tube (tip), pipe extension lines from the cake side to the pastillage triangles. Work around the cake in one direction only first – either right to left or left to right. When complete, repeat the process, piping in the opposite direction. Secure a band of 3mm (⅛ inch) wide ribbon above the pastillage triangles. The ribbon may be attached to the cake before the lines are piped as it is easier to fix it in place at that stage.

4m (4½ yd) × 3mm (⅛ inch) ribbon.

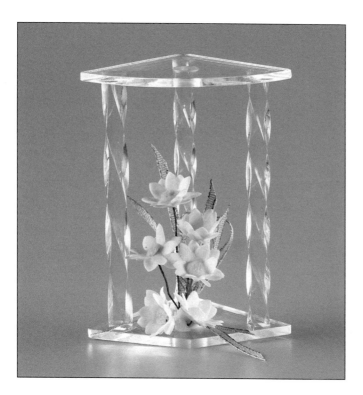

Square cakes have become very popular because they are easy to cut into individual portions.

▲ Place a small ball of sugarpaste on the base of each of the perspex pillars. Arrange the ribbons and flowers in delicate sprays, carefully inserting each wired stem into the paste. Allow to set.

Make 120 daisies and 30 ribbon loops with tails.

▶ The top decoration is a modern perspex stand which follows the triangle shape design. Make an arrangement of daisies and ribbon loops on the stand as for the cake pillars.

1.8m (2 yd) × 3mm (⅛ inch) ribbon for loops.

PERFECT *in* PINK

This three-tier design combines fan-shaped cakes of equal size on a semi-circular board to emphasize their shape. Piped butterflies and sugar Broiderie Anglais lace complement the clever use of pink and white sugarpaste coatings.

SKILLS
~

Double-coating
Broiderie Anglais frill
Brush embroidery
Piped embroidery
Piped shells
Moulded flowers

three 15cm (6 inch) fan-shaped cakes
three 20cm (8 inch) fan-shaped cakes
60cm (24 inch) semi-circular board
straight frill cutter
nos. 1 and 0 piping tubes (tips)

▶ Trim the cakes so that they are all equal in depth, if necessary. Cover with marzipan (almond paste). Coat only the sides of the cakes with white sugarpaste and bevel their top edges. Coat the boards with pink sugarpaste and allow to dry.

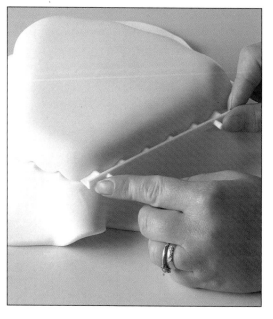

◀ Dampen the cake tops and a little of their sides with clear alcohol. Coat the cakes with pink sugarpaste. Using a straight frill cutter and beginning at the front, cut through the sugarpaste, taking care to keep the cutter straight. Make sure that the pink coating is trimmed in the same place on each tier. Allow to dry for 3 days. Secure the cakes to the boards.

▼ Scribe the butterfly design, see page 156, on the cake tops. Use a no. 1 piping tube (tip) to pipe the scallop loops and the brush-embroidered butterfly wings. Use softened icing to pipe the butterfly bodies and two shells in the form of hearts between each scallop.

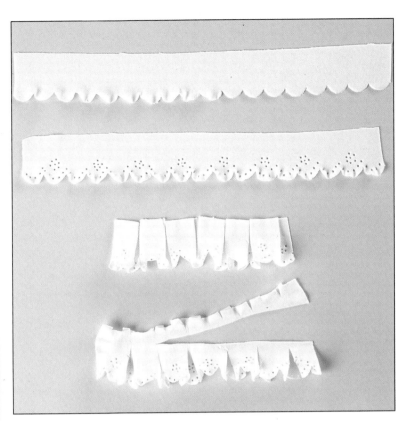

▲ Mix equal portions of flower paste and sugarpaste together. Roll out the paste and cut out a straight frill. Roll the scalloped edge with a cocktail stick, to frill it. Use a no. 1 piping tube (tip) to stamp out small lace holes in the frill. Box pleat the frill, then roll the top edge and trim it level. Use a little egg white to attach the frill to the cake board all around the cake base.

185g (6 oz) each of flower paste and sugarpaste.

◄ Pipe a small shell border around the cake using a no. 1 piping tube (tip). Pipe a drop loop around the edge of the pink paste. Change to a no. 0 piping tube (tip) and pipe the embroidery design, see page 156. Trim the board edge with ribbon.

2.6m (3 yd) picot edge ribbon.

▲ The flowers for the bouquet should be wired into a shower arrangement, including the ribbon loops, blossom and fern leaves. Place a perspex pillar fitted with a posy holder on the board to display the flowers.

Make 10 roses and rosebuds, 12 fern leaves, 15 sprays of blossom, 6 small carnations and 6 frilled pulled flowers.

FROM THIS DAY . . .

An eighteenth century wedding
dress provided the inspiration
for the distinctive, rich embroidery
design on this cake. An abundance of
lush foliage, roses and alstroemeria, arranged
in a garland around the cake stand, creates the
perfect backdrop for the dramatic cake.

SKILLS
~
*Piped embroidery
Piped shells*

small bell-shaped cake
20cm (8 inch) round 6cm
(2½ inch) deep cake
25cm (10 inch) round 7.5cm
(3 inch) deep cake
23cm (9 inch), 28cm (11 inch)
and 33cm (13 inch) round
boards
nos. 3 and 1 piping tubes (tips)
3 mini deco oasis
40cm (16 inch) fresh oasis ring
cake stand

Coat the cakes with marzipan
(almond paste). Cover the
cakes and boards with peach-
coloured sugarpaste and
allow them to dry for 3 days.
Secure the cakes to the
boards.

▲ Cut a paper template the
height and length of the side
of each of the round cakes;
fold into eight equal sections.
Prepare a similar template for
the lower edge of the bell
cake. Trace the design on
page 156 onto the paper,
adjusting the size for each tier.
Scribe the pattern on the
cakes. Soften some peach

sugarpaste to a piping consistency with water. Using a no. 3 piping tube (tip), pipe a shell border around the cake bases using the softened paste. This will give a perfect colour match. Trim the board edge with ribbon.

2.6m (3 yd) × 5mm (¼ inch) picot edge ribbon.

Pipe the embroidery using a no. 1 piping tube (tip) and royal icing. Mix white lustre colour and clear piping gel and pipe the pearl effect beads in the embroidery.

▶ Place the mini deco oasis on an inverted glass. Insert the foliage stems to build up the shape and size of the bouquet.

▼ Add the flowers, inserting some flowers deep into the arrangement to give it depth. It is important to create a bouquet which looks full but not crowded. Make bouquets for the three cakes: notice the different shapes required for the bell-shaped and round cakes. Measure the length of the bell over the top to get some idea of how long to cut and wire the first pieces of foliage.

► Use a knife to round off the edges of the fresh oasis ring, then soak it in water. Insert the stems of the foliage at an angle, creating a good, even shape.

▼ Arrange gypsophila and alstroemeria around two-thirds of the ring, adding several different types of foliage as background material. Insert the spray of roses and gypsophila, leaving their stems slightly longer so that they stand out as a beautiful focal point. Spray lightly with water.

Attach the assembled bouquets with royal icing.

ORCHID PEARL

Simply, yet exotic, this three-tier
wedding cake is adorned with
beautiful sugar orchids and
trimmed with pearl drops.
Pale pink sugarpaste and delicate gypsophila
sprays ensure the design is light and romantic.

SKILLS
~
Embossing
Piped embroidery
Moulded flowers

13cm (5 inch) hexagonal
5.5cm (2½ inch) deep cake
20cm (8 inch) hexagonal
6cm (2½ inch) deep cake
28cm (11 inch) hexagonal
7.5cm (3 inch) deep cake
13cm (5 inch), 20cm (8 inch)
and 28cm (11 inch) thin
boards
20cm (8 inch), 28cm (11 inch)
and 36cm (14 inch) hexagonal
boards
nos. 1 and 0 piping tubes (tips)
embossing tool or suitable
button
straight 'E' stand

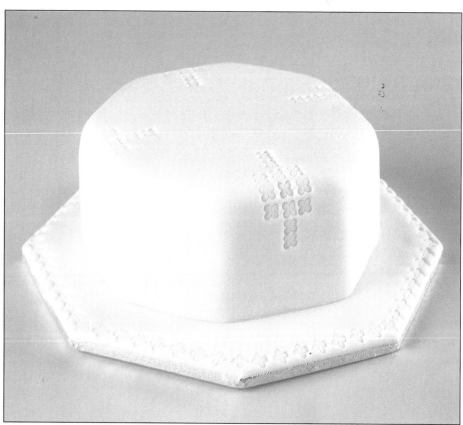

▲ Place the cakes on thin
boards cut to their exact sizes
and coat with marzipan
(almond paste). Coat the cake
boards with shell pink
sugarpaste. Use a decorative
button or embossing tool to
emboss the edges of the
boards. Allow to dry. Coat
the cakes with shell pink sugarpaste and emboss alternate
sides of the tops. Secure the
cakes to the prepared boards.
Allow to dry.

► Using a no. 1 piping tube (tip), pipe royal icing around the cake base to secure the 1cm (½ inch) wide lustre ribbon. Pipe short lines of icing above the ribbon and attach the strung pearl drops. Support the pearls with pins until the icing has dried. Remove the pins.

2.6m (3 yd) strung pearl drops.

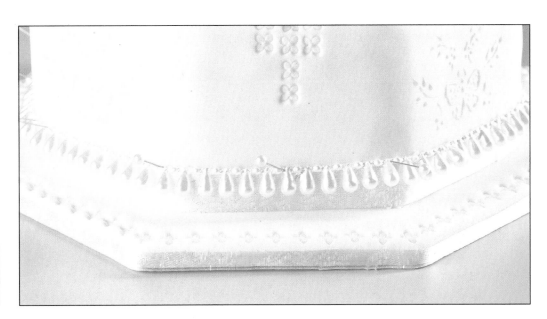

◄ Trace the pattern, see page 157, and scribe it onto the four sides of the cake which have not been embossed. Mix white lustre colour with clear piping jelly. Using a no. 0 piping tube (tip) pipe the embroidery. Pipe a dot in the centre of each embossed floret to resemble a pearl.

► Wire three bouquets, each with three orchids, two figure-of-eight bows, two sprays of pearl loops and gypsophila. Cut the stems to 3.5cm (1½ inch). Secure to cake with softened flower paste; hold in place with hat pins until set. Trim boards with half-width ribbon.

9 Cymbidium orchids, bunch of dried gypsophila, 12 sprays of pearl loops and 6.3m (7 yd) × 1cm (½ inch) lustre ribbon.

A WINTER WEDDING

A colour scheme of brilliant red, festive green and celebration gold makes this a magical wedding cake for the Christmas season.

10cm (4 inch) round 5cm
(2 inch) deep cake
14cm (5½ inch) round 5.5cm
(2¼ inch) deep cake
16.5cm (6¾ inch) round 6cm
(2½ inch) deep cake
20cm (8 inch) round 6.5cm
(2¾ inch) deep cake
23cm (9 inch) round 7.5cm
(3 inch) deep cake
10cm (4 inch), 14cm (5½ inch),
16.5cm (6¾ inch), 20cm
(8 inch) and 23cm (9 inch)
thin boards
airbrushing equipment
nos. 1 and 0 piping tubes (tips)
left five-tier perspex stand

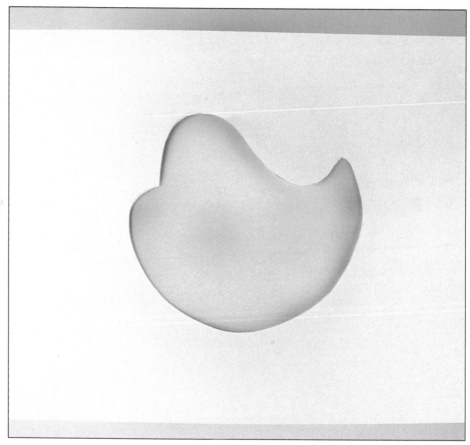

▲ Place the cakes on thin boards cut to their exact sizes and coat them with marzipan (almond paste). Coat with white sugarpaste and leave to dry for 5 days. Adjust the heart pattern on page 157 to fit each of the cakes. Draw the hearts on large pieces of paper and use a scalpel to cut them out, keeping the surrounding paper whole.

▶ Place the paper heart on the cake and hold it in place with coins. Next, position the surrounding paper from which the heart shape was cut. Move the coins on it, placing them near the cake edge. Carefully remove the central heart pattern. The cut-out heart shape is now correctly positioned and ready to be sprayed with green liquid food colouring using an aerograph (airbrush).

◀ Cut a paper template for the side of the cake. Fold the paper into eight equal sections. Cut out the scallop pattern, retaining the top part. Position the top half of the template around the cake and spray the lower area with green food colouring.

◀ Protect the top of the cake with paper, then turn it upside down. Pipe royal icing on the base edge and attach the lace trimming.

3.2m (3½ yd) × 2.5cm (1 inch) gathered lace.

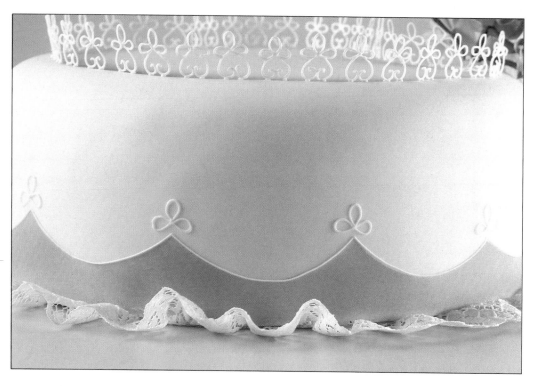

◄Using a no. 1 piping tube (tip), pipe a drop loop over the airbrush line on the side of the cake. Pipe a trefoil shape at the top of each scallop to match the top of the lace.

Use a no. 0 piping tube (tip) to pipe lace pieces from both sizes of design, see page 157. Insert a posy holder into the curve of each heart. Attach the lace pieces with dots of royal icing around the heart shape.

Make 150 lace pieces of each size.

► Wire the flowers into bouquets graduated in size for the cakes. Place a small piece of flower paste in each posy holder to prevent the bouquets moving and damaging the piped lace. Then position the bouquets and allow to set before moving the cakes.

Make 5 pointsettia of graduated size, 50 winter forsythia, 80 holly leaves and berries.

SIMPLY STUNNING

A simple design is essential for a buttercream-coated cake to complete immediately before the wedding. This is ideal for those who want an alternative to fruit cake and royal icing or sugarpaste.

SKILLS
~
*Cut-out lace border
Piped shells*

15cm (6 inch) round 5cm
(2 inch) deep genoese sponge
20cm (8 inch) round 6cm
(2½ inch) deep genoese sponge
25cm (10 inch) round 7.5cm
(3 inch) deep genoese sponge
20cm (8 inch), 25cm (10 inch)
and 33cm (13 inch) round
boards
lace cutter
no. 6 piping tube (tip)
'S' stand

▶ Cut the cakes into 1cm (½ inch) layers using guide sticks to ensure that each layer is evenly deep. Slice three layers for the top tier and four layers for the bottom and middle tiers. Sandwich the cakes back together with lemon curd or jam and buttercream flavoured to your requirements.

Coat each tier with buttercream. Place the cakes in the freezer until firm but do not freeze the coating until it is solid as condensation will form on the surface when the cake is removed from the freezer. Apply a second coat to the cakes and use a hot metal side scraper and straight edge to achieve a smooth finish.

Buttercream
To make the buttercream, gradually beat 500g (1 lb/ 3 cups) sifted icing (confectioners') sugar into 1kg (2 lb) unsalted butter. Add 2 teaspoons natural vanilla essence (extract) and continue beating until the mixture is soft and pale. Beat in a little evaporated milk to soften the buttercream to a good piping consistency. Taste for flavour and add more vanilla if required.

▶ Cut the lace border from sugarpaste and attach it to the sides of the cakes. Take care to roll the sugarpaste to the same thickness as you cut each section of the border. Using a no. 6 piping tube (tip), pipe a shell border around the top and bottom edges of each cake.

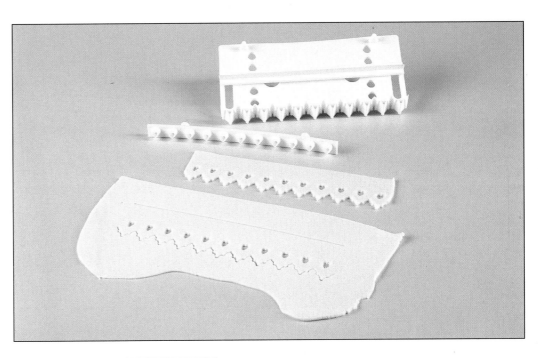

250g (½ lb) peach-coloured sugarpaste.

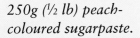

◀ Wire each ivy leaf and freesia and tape them with floristry tape to help preserve the flowers. Make two returns on each bouquet for each part of the cake stand. Tape the flowers to the stand with floristry tape. The wired stems should overlap the stand at the centre point to form beautiful flowing bouquets of flowers.

40 stems of cream freesia; variegated ivy.

SIMPLY STUNNING

TOGETHER *for* EVER

Simply sophisticated, this two-tier
heart-shaped cake, delicately piped with
embroidery and crowned with a bouquet
of fresh flowers, is a perpetual favourite.

SKILLS
~
Comb-scraped coating
Piped embroidery
Oriental string work

15cm (6 inch) heart-shaped
6cm (2½ inch) deep cake
25cm (10 inch) heart-shaped
7.5cm (3 inch) deep cake
15cm (6 inch) and 25cm
(10 inch) heart-shaped thin
boards
23cm (9 inch) and 36cm
(14 inch) heart-shaped boards
nos. 0 and 1 piping tubes (tips)
1 mini deco oasis
length of perspex tube for
flowers
3 round perspex pillars

▲ Place the cakes on thin
boards cut to their exact size
and cover with marzipan
(almond paste). Coat the
cakes with royal icing. Use a
comb scraper on the final side
coat to mark the line design.

Secure the cakes to the coated
boards and trim the board
edges with lace.

2.2m (2½ yd) lace.

► Cut a heart-shaped paper template the size of the top of the coated cake. Fold the paper in half and draw the scallop design, then cut out the shape. Place the template on the cake, then use a no. 0 piping tube (tip) to pipe short lines around each scallop and the embroidery, see page 157. It is important not to scribe any pencil marks on this cake as it would be impossible to cover them.

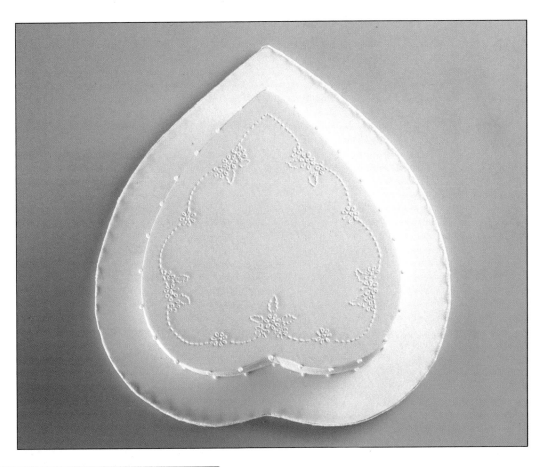

◄Using dividers set at 1.5cm (¾ inch), mark the top edge starting at the front point for each side. Adjust the size of each space slightly to fit towards the back if necessary. Repeat for the bottom edge. Using a no. 1 piping tube (tip) and softened royal icing pipe a dot on each division mark.

◄Use royal icing to attach the bands of 3mm (⅛ inch) ribbon between the comb scraped lines on the sides of the cakes. Pipe the embroidery using a no. 0 piping tube (tip).

3.2m (2½ yd) × 3mm (⅛ inch) ribbon.

▶ Place a firm piece of sponge/foam on the middle of the cake top – not over the embroidery. Then turn the cake upside down. Using a no. 1 piping tube (tip), pipe three rows of drop loops from the piped dots around the top and bottom edge. Allow to dry, then turn the cake back over.

◀ Secure a perspex tube to the top-tier board with royal icing – this is for the flowers. Tape the flowers into a bouquet and spray them with water to keep them fresh until they are placed in position on the assembled cake.

Fresh flowers: 3 lilies, 3 lily buds, 9 wired ivy leaves, 5 wired alstroemeria, 3 sprays of freesia and 6 wired leaves.

CHOCOLATE DREAM

This two-tier chocolate cake filled
with dairy cream and fresh strawberries
is as luscious to eat as it is beautiful
to look at. Whipped white chocolate
ganache is used to coat and decorate
the cakes and fresh strawberries
make up the top-piece arrangement.

SKILLS
~
Piped roses
Miniature scrolls
Herringbone piping
Moulded flowers

15cm (6 inch) round 5cm
(2 inch) deep chocolate cake
30 × 25cm (12 × 10 inch)
elongated hexagonal 6cm
(2½ inch) deep chocolate cake
18cm (7 inch) round board
38 × 33cm (15 × 13 inch)
elongated hexagonal board
2kg (4 lb) white chocolate
1.25 litres (40 fl oz/5 cups)
whipping cream
625ml (20 fl oz/2½ cups)
double (heavy) cream
500g (1 lb/1½ cups) strawberry
preserve
1kg (2 lb) strawberries
nos. 3 and 2 piping tubes (tips)

To make the ganache, melt
the white chocolate in a large
bowl over a saucepan of hot
water. Boil half the whipping
cream with the double cream.
Slowly beat the cream into
the chocolate, then cool and
refrigerate overnight.

▲ Cut four layers of chocolate
cake for the bottom tier and
three layers of cake for the
top tier, using 1cm (½ inch)
guide sticks to ensure that the
cake is cut evenly.

▶ Whip the remaining whipping cream until thick. Layer the cakes with strawberry preserve, whipped cream and sliced strawberries. Ensure that the assembled cake is level by placing a cake board on the top and applying even pressure to it.

Place the cakes on the cake boards. Beat the ganache thoroughly, then use it to coat the cakes completely but not too thickly. Refrigerate until firm, then give the cakes a second coat of ganache. Use a hot metal side scraper and straight edge to achieve a smooth surface.

The fresh strawberries cascading from each tier indicate the type of filling in this beautiful, contemporary wedding cake.

◀ Place chocolate and cream-coloured ribbon-threaded lace around the middle of the cake sides. Use a no. 3 piping tube (tip) to pipe ropes of ganache around the bottom edge of the cake. Overpipe using a no. 2 piping tube (tip).

2.2m (2½ yd) ribbon-threaded lace.

► Use the point of a knife to mark the hexagonal shape on top of the bottom tier, 3.5cm (1½ inch) inside the edge. Use a no. 2 piping (tip) to pipe 'S' and 'C' scrolls along the mark. Pipe a herringbone shell border around the top edge of each tier.

► Roll out a long rope of flower paste and taper each end to a point. Shape to form a 'C', see page 157. Cut out a small triangle of flower paste and allow to dry. Soften a small ball of flower paste, place it on the disc and position the 'C' shape.

About 125g (4 oz/¼ lb) flower paste.

► Make twelve sugar strawberry flowers. Place a small piece of sugarpaste on the bottom tier. Build up a bouquet using wired fresh strawberry leaves, fresh strawberries and sugar flowers. Place a piece of sugarpaste on the 'C' stand before positioning it on the top tier. Make an arrangement of leaves, flowers and strawberries in the sugarpaste to trail over the edge of the top-tier cake.

12 sugar strawberry flowers.

PILLARS AND STANDS

There is a wide choice of cake stands and pillars on which to display wedding cakes. Many options are shown throughout this book but the possibilities are even greater – subject only to your imagination and ability to make as well as hire stands.

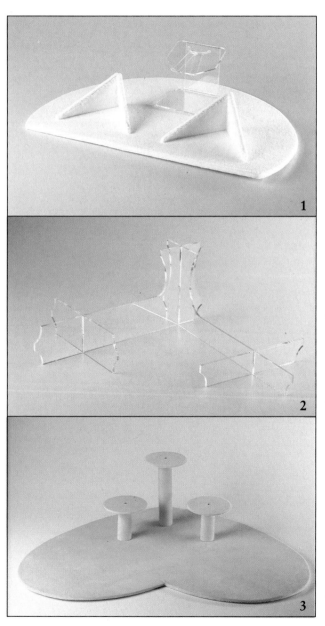

Pillars are available in plastic, chalk or perspex. If they are used on a cake covered with sugarpaste, or soft coating, the tiers have to be reinforced with wooden dowels to support the pillars and prevent the cake collapsing. Mark the positions for the pillars on the bottom and middle tiers. Cut four pieces of wooden dowel of equal length for each tier: they must be slightly longer than the combined measurement of the cake depth and pillar. Insert the dowel through the cake taking care to ensure that it is straight. Hollow pillars are then placed over the dowel. When using solid pillars cut the dowel level with the cake coating. If the cake is not perfectly level place thin discs of pastillage under the pillars. Check using a spirit level.

Stands
Cake stands are available for hire from cake decorating or catering suppliers and the hire charge often includes the decorative cake knife for the ceremonial cutting.
Perspex and chrome stands are attractive and versatile. They have the advantage of supporting the cakes without having to use dowel rods and they dispense with the danger of the cake collapsing.

Stands can be used for cakes of various designs and with any coating – experiment yourself by alternating the design and choice of stand to produce different effects.

Home-made Stands
Beautiful stands can be made to your exact requirements. Cut different lengths of wooden dowel and cover them with fabric to complement the wedding colours or theme. Secure the dowel to a large covered board. Experiment with different heights and arrangements but make sure that the boards are secure and sufficiently solid to take the weight of the decorated cakes.

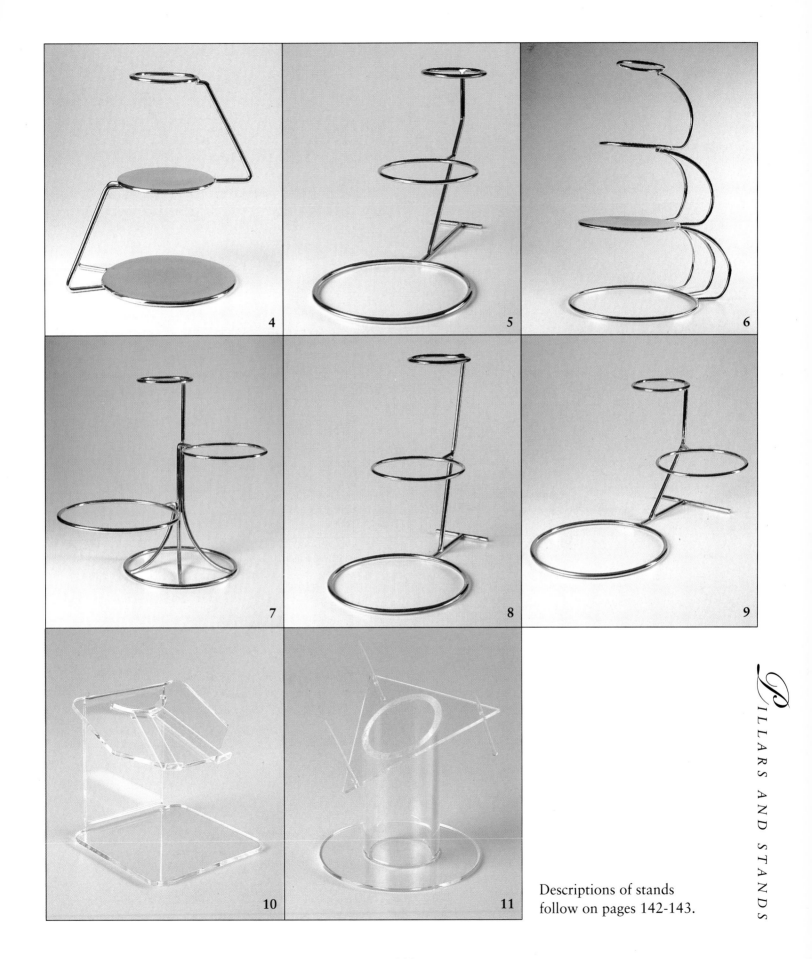

4

5

6

7

8

9

10

11

Descriptions of stands
follow on pages 142-143.

141

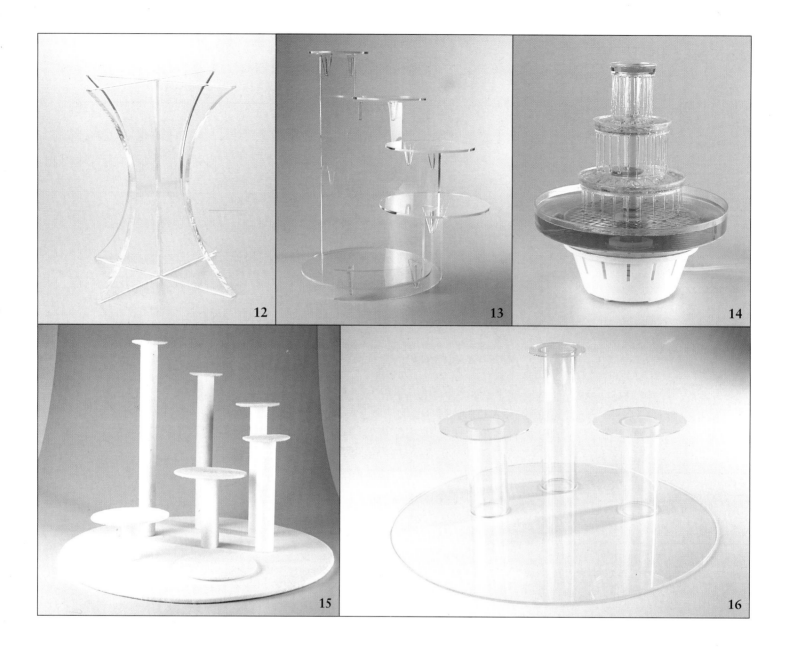

A VARIETY OF DESIGNS FOR PILLARS AND STANDS

1 Triangles of plywood are hinged together at the back, covered and placed on a covered plywood base. The purchased perspex stand provides a higher platform for a three tier cake.

2 An adaptable perspex stand in kit form to display one to three tiers in a number of ways.

3 Another example of a home-made stand: three small cake boards are screwed securely onto three lengths of dowel which are screwed onto a plywood base. Each section is covered with velvet, discreetly stitched in place, before the stand is assembled.

4 Three-tier chrome stand which can be adjusted into an 'E' shape if required. Also available with a fourth tier attachment.

5 Low staggered chrome stand with angled arm between upper tiers, allowing bouquets to be draped from one tier to the next.

6 This stand may be dismantled to display one to four tiers. The chrome hoop on the top may be used to display a top decoration or bouquet over a single tier cake. The stand may be twisted into an 'S' shape.

7 Three-tier chrome tree stand which allows space for the bridal bouquet and bridesmaids' posies to be arranged around the base at the reception.

8 A basic, high staggered stand of simple design. Ideal for the beginner to use, as it supports cakes well. The design ensures that the cakes do not overshadow tiers below.

9 Three-tier, stainless steel off-set step stand.

10 An alternative tilting cake stand. This is not designed for large or heavy cakes as the perspex tends to flex and bounce slightly.

11 This tilting stand takes one cake which may be the top tier displayed with one or two other cakes in a lower arrangement beside it. The perspex spikes are intended for piercing the board and cake to hold it in place. However it can be quite difficult to push these into the cake. As an alternative, I attached a plastic angle to the base of the cake board, see page 26.

12 A clear perspex stand which slots together. This may be used to display the top tier or a single tier cake. It also makes a useful platform to give extra height to a top decoration.

13 This stand is one of a pair of mirror image stands. It is a fragile stand with removable disks which hold the cakes. Ideal for light cakes with soft coatings, such as fresh cream or buttercream. The stand supports the cakes well and, being completely washable, it is also a hygienic choice.

14 An electric fountain filled with coloured water. An additional attachment can be added to create a different water flow. An arrangement of flowers may be used to conceal the white base.

15 A seven-tier stand created from boards screwed to cylinders. All the pieces are covered with stretch velour before they are assembled. The cylinders or pillars are not permanently fixed, allowing for the arrangement to be altered. The cakes may be displayed in a spiral form, as here, or the tallest cylinder can be placed in the middle allowing for a cascade of cakes.

16 Perspex tubes and disks of polished-edge perspex make up this simple stand. The tubes and disks are not fixed to allow for the display to be varied. Also, if the tubes are fixed, then condensation tends to collect inside, clouding the perspex and this is impossible to clean.

CREATING THE PERFECTLY BALANCED DISPLAY

Care must be taken to create a cake which is not only a safe structure but also visually well balanced.

A tiered cake, including the top decoration, should fit into an imaginary triangle. The cakes should look equal in depth when assembled but to achieve this the bottom tier must be deeper than the top tier to prevent the smallest cake looking top heavy.

Using pillars which are slightly smaller between the top and middle tiers, and taller pillars between the middle and bottom tiers will also help the overall balance.

The top piece on the cake should fit into the overall triangular shape and design. The exact position and arrangement must be planned in advance so that the cake tiers are perfectly complemented when assembled. This book illustrates a variety of top pieces and decorations. With careful attention to the overall design these can be interchanged to suit individual tastes and themes, and still result in a stunning cake.

Complicated pastillage top pieces may be created using the strengthening technique described for the spire on St Paul's Church, see page 64. An overlay of rolled-out pastillage is placed over the cut and arrange sections. This is stuck in place and trimmed to allow for easy and flexible assembly of curved constructions.

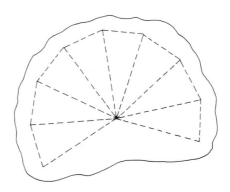

143

TEMPLATES

Wedding Romance, *see page 8*

Enchantment, *see page 20*

Elegance, *see page 24*

Crystal Tiers, *see page 28*

Elegance, *see page 24*

Extension work pattern

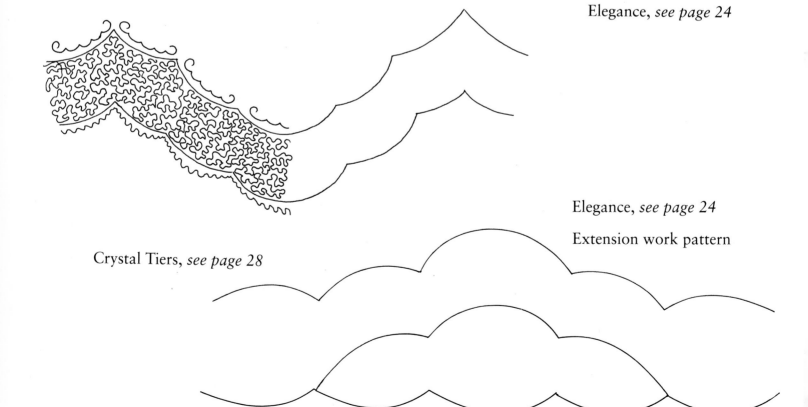

Wedding Day, *see page 40*

Top decoration

Top decoration

Classic Embroidery,
see page 32

Enlarge all templates on pages 144/145 by 123 per cent on a photocopier.

145

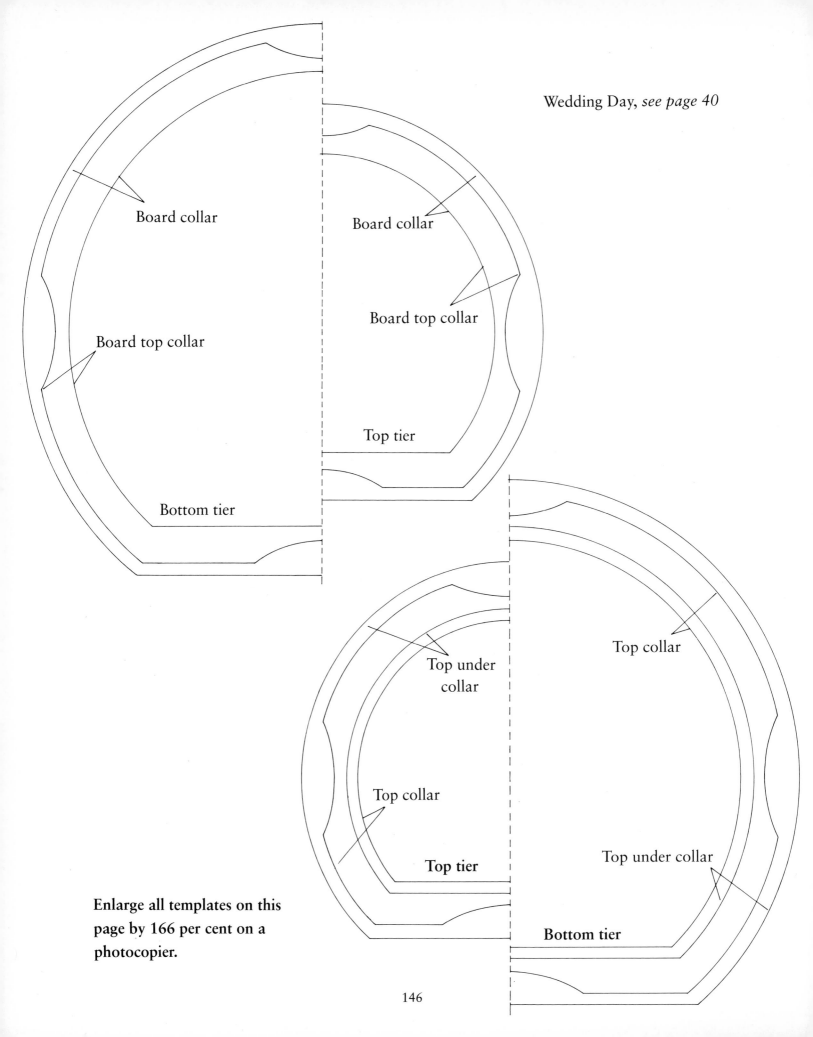

Board collar

Board collar

Board top collar

Board top collar

Top tier

Bottom tier

Wedding Day, *see page 40*

Top under collar

Top collar

Top collar

Top tier

Top under collar

Bottom tier

Enlarge all templates on this page by 166 per cent on a photocopier.

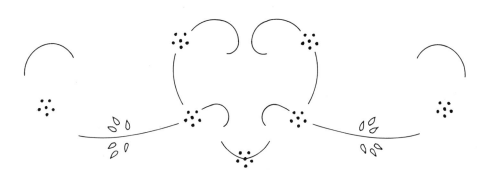

Sweet Hearts, *see page 60*

Spring Garlands, *see page 44*

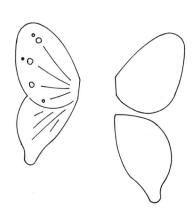

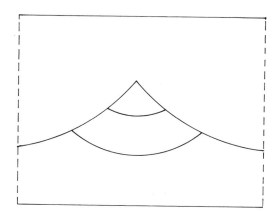

With This Ring, *see page 48*

Be Mine For Ever, *see page 56*

Enlarge all templates on this page by 123 per cent on a photocopier.

Bells of Joy, *see page 52*

Templates on this page shown actual size.

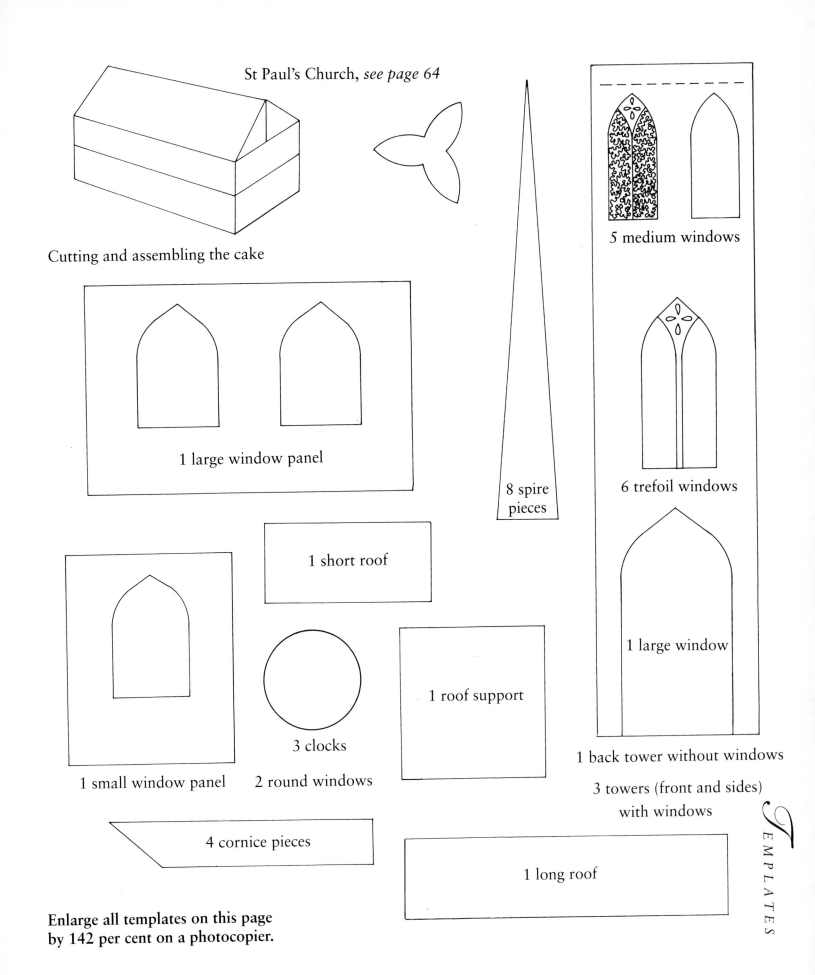

St Paul's Church, *see page 64*

Cutting and assembling the cake

1 large window panel

5 medium windows

8 spire pieces

6 trefoil windows

1 short roof

1 roof support

1 large window

3 clocks

1 small window panel   2 round windows

1 back tower without windows

3 towers (front and sides) with windows

4 cornice pieces

1 long roof

Enlarge all templates on this page by 142 per cent on a photocopier.

Roses for Susan, *see page 68*

Enlarge all templates on this page by 112 per cent on a photocopier.

Bluebirds of Love, *see page 72*

1 top collar

1 bottom collar

1 top base collar

Note: make extra pieces to allow for breakages

Enlarge all templates on this page by 123 per cent on a photocopier.

Bluebirds of Love, *see page 72*

4 side panels

4 front side panels

Top

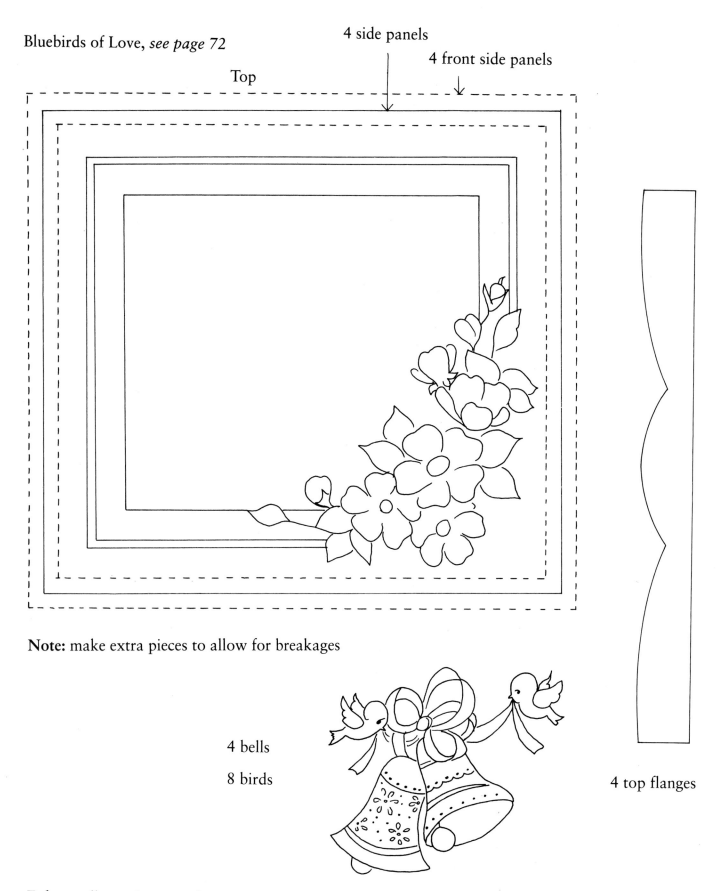

Note: make extra pieces to allow for breakages

4 bells

8 birds

4 top flanges

Enlarge all templates on this page by 123 per cent on a photocopier.

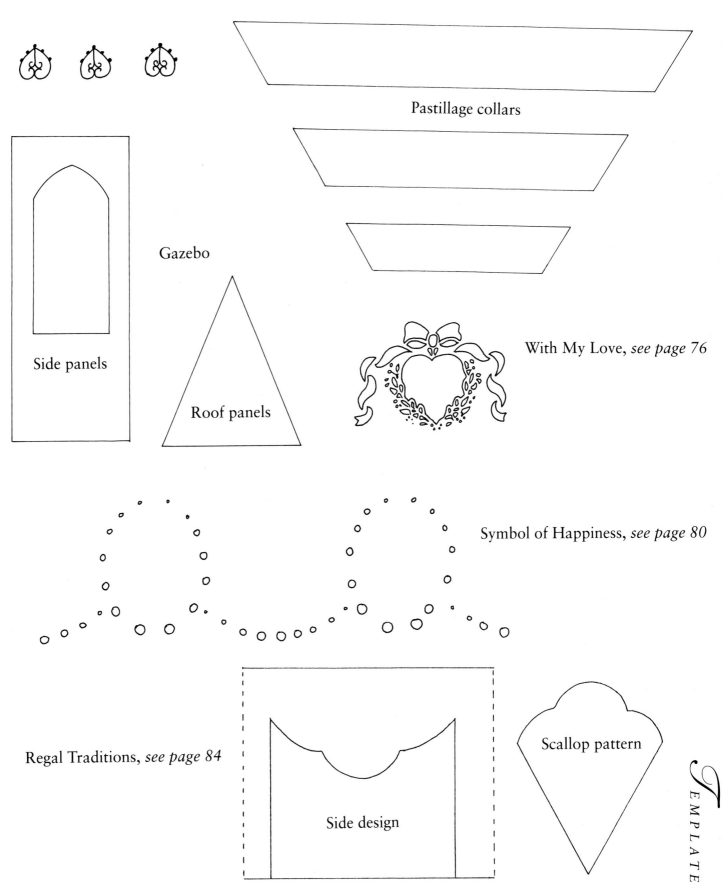

Pastillage collars

Gazebo

Side panels

Roof panels

With My Love, *see page 76*

Symbol of Happiness, *see page 80*

Regal Traditions, *see page 84*

Side design

Scallop pattern

Enlarge all templates on this page by 123 per cent on a photocopier.

Forget-Me-Not, *see page 100*

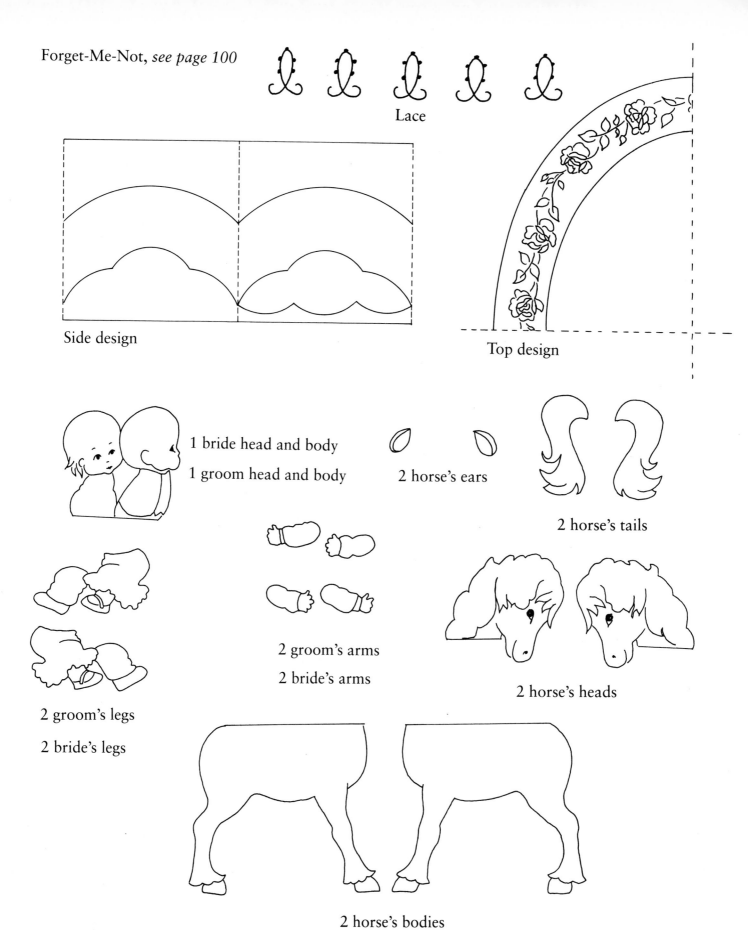

Lace

Side design

Top design

1 bride head and body

1 groom head and body

2 horse's ears

2 horse's tails

2 groom's arms

2 bride's arms

2 horse's heads

2 groom's legs

2 bride's legs

2 horse's bodies

Enlarge all templates on this page by 142 per cent on a photocopier.

Bouquet Cascade, *see page 92*

Dream Maker, *see page 96*

Figures

Side design

Wedgwood Blue, *see page 104*

Top design

Enlarge all templates on this page by 123 per cent on a photocopier.

Spring Wedding, *see page 108*

Perfect in Pink, *see page 112*

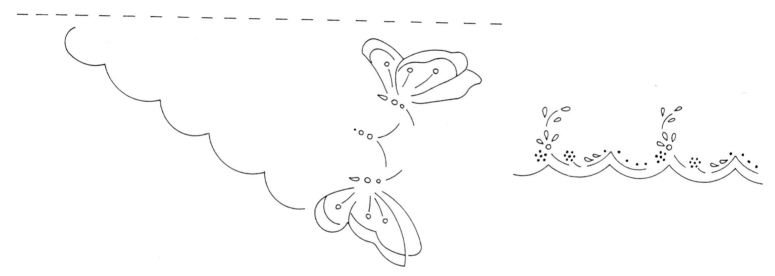

From This Day . . . , *see page 116*

Enlarge all templates on this page by 123 per cent on a photocopier.

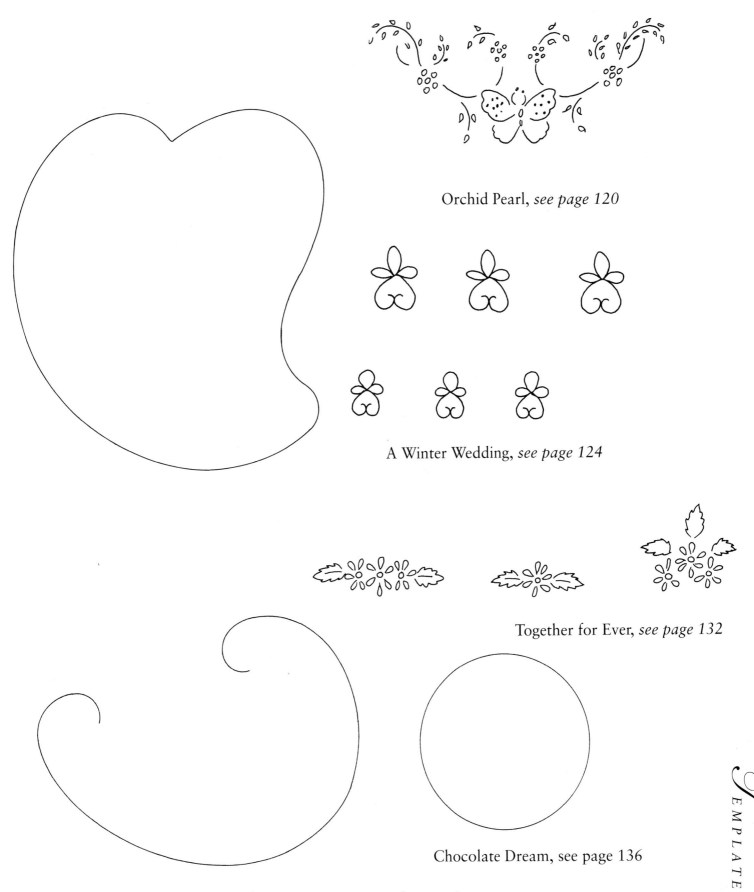

Orchid Pearl, *see page 120*

A Winter Wedding, *see page 124*

Together for Ever, *see page 132*

Chocolate Dream, see page 136

Enlarge all templates on this page by 112 per cent on a photocopier.

INDEX

ACKNOWLEDGEMENTS

The author and publishers would like to thank the following for their assistance:

Angela's, 2 Woodlands Close, Kadoma, Zimbabwe

A.O.K. Metals, 16 Queensland Road, Bournemouth BH5 2AB

Cake Art, Unit 16, Crown Close, Crown Industrial Estate, Priorswood, Taunton, Somerset TA2 8RX

Cel Cakes, Springfield House, Gate Helmsley, York YO4 1NF

Craigmillar, Craigmillar House, Stadium Road, Bromborough, Wirral, Merseyside L62 3NU

Domino Plastics, Unit 4, Blenheim Court, Wickford Essex SS11 8YT

House of Cake, 18 Meadow Close, Woodley, Stockport, Cheshire SK6 1QZ

J.F. Renshaw Ltd., Mitcham House, Surrey GU21 5RP

Orchard Products, 51 Hallyburton Road, Hove, East Sussex BN3 7GP

Rainbow Ribbons, Seedbed Centre, Romford, Essex

Squires Kitchen, 3 Waverley Lane, Farnham GU9 8BB

Twins, 67-69 Victoria Road, Romford, Essex RM1 2LT

Special thanks are due to the following for their kind help: Liz and Austin O'Koye (A.O.K. Metals),
Margaret and David Ford (Cel Cakes), Pat and George Ashby (Orchard Products),
Rita Snelling (Rainbow Ribbons), Beverley (Squires Kitchen) and Jean Dillon and Joan Shaw (Twins).

FOR FURTHER INFORMATION

Merehurst is the leading publisher of cake decorating books and has an excellent range of titles to suit cake decorators of all levels. Please send for a free catalogue, stating the title of this book:

United Kingdom
Marketing Department
Merehurst Ltd.
Ferry House
51-57 Lacy Road
London SW15 1PR

Tel: 081 780 1177
Fax: 081 780 1714

U.S.A./Canada
Foxwood International Ltd.
150 Nipissing Rd. 6
Milton
Ontario
L9T 5B2 Canada

Tel: (1) 905 875 4040
Fax: (1) 905 875 1668

Australia
J.B. Fairfax Ltd.
80 McLachlan Avenue
Rushcutters Bay
NSW 2011

Tel: (61) 2 361 6366
Fax: (61) 2 360 6262

Other Territories For further information contact:
International Sales Department at United Kingdom address.